CONTROLLING THE PAUSE

Reusable Tools
for Leaders in
Big Transition

KRISTIN RINK VOTTA

ADVANCE PRAISE FOR *CONTROLLING THE PAUSE*

Every business leader, whether in transition or not can profit from this book's simple approach. Take a moment to examine: are you making a difference, and are you achieving all you can? If not, why not? If you're a high achiever, then this book is for you. You have likely read a lot of books, but none allow you to cut through the voice in your head to see a way forward quite like this book.

– Michelle Gemalsky,
VP Fortune 50 Company

As a leader of multiple groups and organizations for over 40 years I can say with certainty that the only constant for leaders is that people and organizations change and evolve. Managing that evolution in a way that is beneficial to both the bottom line and its people is the ultimate challenge of leadership. With this book and the Votta Exercise, Kristin has given us a value-based tool kit to enable us to create a high-performance culture. I highly recommend this book and process to anyone committed to making their organization and the lives of their people better.

– David Forrester,
serial entrepreneur

The world becomes less complicated having leveraged The Votta Exercise. Kristin succeeds in shaking up our views, challenging our observations, and perhaps most important: changing our behavior.

– Sarah Sweeny,
Product LifeCycle and Brand Strategy,
Fortune 500 Company

Kristin's powerful, perceptive, and practical advice unpacks the complex challenges we face every day and provides resources that empower the reader to lean in to the most uncomfortable situations. As we all grapple with how to make our workplaces more inclusive, this book is a must-read for leaders of all levels.

– **Crysta Dungee,**
Global Inclusion and Diversity Leader,
Fortune 10 Company

I have witnessed Kristin's ability firsthand to make a profound and lasting change in the culture of a non-profit during a period of big transition. Kristin not only provided tools for the organization's leadership, she empowered them with the skills necessary to inspire and motivate their teams to achieve significant results moving forward on an ongoing basis.

– **Ailen Cruz,**
Esq.

"Pause like you mean it" implores a candy bar jingle. This book is for all leaders who mean it. Leaders who are serious about and inspired to achieve their vision, mission, strategy, goal, or objective. The path to get there is sometimes unclear or blocked, and this book contains powerful and very practical approaches to remove the block and get us moving forward in a variety of circumstances. *Controlling the Pause: Reusable Tools for Leaders in Big Transition* is the next best thing to spending the day with Kristin. Both she and her book leave one feeling lighter, more capable, and better equipped to get it done, and done well.

– **Edna Katherine Morris,**
Restaurateur, Investor

Editor: Karen Rowe, www.karenrowe.com
Cover Design: Shake Creative, ShakeTampa.com
Author image: Mike Ossola, Mike Ossola Photography
Inside Layout: Ljiljana Pavkov

Printed in the United States

ISBN: 978-1-64999-510-0 (paperback)

ISBN: 978-1-64999-511-7 (eBook)

To Annabella and Dylan,

Thank you for showing me that a pandemic is just an excuse to play together more often, for helping me pick out my "bossy lady" outfits for virtual meetings, and for reminding me that I, too, feel better after laughing, crying, and/or screaming as loud as humanly possible. I love you and your dad more than I could ever promise.

"The task of leadership is not to put greatness into humanity, but to elicit it, for the greatness is already there."

– J. Buchan

Table of

Contents

Introduction • What Is the "Pause"?.................................... 13

Chapter 1 • The Votta Exercise Origin Story 17

Chapter 2 • Step One: Pick a Personal Goal or Issue ...27

   Paul's Story—Managing People for the First Time ... 28

Chapter 3 • Step Two: Separate the Facts from
Your View 35

   A Personal Example—Expanding My Business 38
   Anna's Story—Pursuing the Next Promotion 40
   Working Through Transitions 43

Chapter 4 • Step Three: Choose a View 45

   Gabriel's Story—Making Money Even During
     a Recession 48
   Vincent 's Story—Doubling Sales Targets 49
   Reframing Mistakes 52

Chapter 5 • Step Four: Look Back 55

   Allison's Story—Advancing a Career After 14 Years 60
   In the Face of Failure 62

Chapter 6 • Step Five: Look Ahead 65

   How to Create a Plan 68

Forcing Success 70
Structures with Personality Assessments 72
Feedback Structures 73
Maya's Story—Creating a Legacy 75
Structures to Measure Views 76
Maria's Story—Intentional Downsizing 77

Chapter 7 • Step Six: Reevaluate
(The Bigger Picture) 83

Amber's Story—Creating New Services 85
Vision and Mission 88
The Opportunity of Leadership Retreats 89
A Note on Equity, Equality, Diversity,
    and Inclusion 92
Reassessing Employee Recruitment
    and Retention 95
Using Transitions to Pause and Reevaluate 97

Chapter 8 • Coaching Others through the Exercise 101

Don't Give Advice 101
Check in Regularly 103
Handling Perfectionism 104
Working with Family 107
Don't Make Assumptions 110
Setting Boundaries 111
Intentionally Look for Things to Appreciate 116

Creating the Life You Want 121

Acknowledgements 123

About the Author 127

Notes 129

CONTROLLING
THE PAUSE

Introduction

What Is the "Pause"?

I trust you are coming to this book with some self-awareness, maybe even a lot. I also assume you were drawn or led here because you're going through a transition—a "pause"—in your life or career that has left you feeling a bit stuck. You know you need help; a new tool, perhaps, to help you climb out of the muck of conflicting thoughts or self-limiting beliefs. You are the kind of person who has used tools effectively in the past, and maybe even worked with consultants or coaches in various personal or work-related situations. You are used to keeping an open mind, and you are used to getting results.

Maybe transitions have normally been easy for you—not that you haven't had to work to get through them, but hard work has never scared you. You have likely worked hard for everything in your life, and that hard work has almost always paid off. Results have often turned out in your favor, but right now they are not.

Maybe this is the first time in your life where things are not working out. Maybe you didn't get that promotion. Perhaps you took an early retirement package; you thought you would enjoy retirement, but you are not. Or, maybe you were laid off, and securing the next opportunity is taking longer than expected. Maybe a transition into the industry you want to go into isn't coming easily. You might be coming to this book frustrated, and surprised that you are frustrated. You have done it before—whatever *it* is. Why isn't it going the same *this* time?

It is also possible there has been no pause at all, but you are intentionally looking to grow or add a new tool to your leadership development "library".

We can all likely agree that we are living in unprecedented times. Maybe you think external factors—a pandemic, the market, or the economy—have had an impact in terms of how things have changed in your life. If that is you, I can assure you, using external factors to explain what is happening is a normal excuse. I won't use the word *excuse* anywhere else in the rest of this book. That said, I use it here to make my point. A lot of people see external crises as reasons for their current situation. But there are always crises. Depending on one's perspective, or what I call "view," one could say we have *always* lived in unprecedented times. What I seek to do with this book is to show that how we view external factors has an enormous impact on our success. I do this using the Votta Exercise™.

The Votta Exercise is a six-step method I use with my coaching clients—leaders from as large as Fortune 10 companies, entrepreneurs, nonprofit executives, and more—to achieve new results. I started my business, Votta Coaching and Consulting in 2018, but I have been coaching leaders and facilitating seminars for over sixteen years. Time and again, I see my clients overcome obstacles, including big transitions or "pauses" in their lives, by separating *facts* from their personal views, and using that new awareness to shift perspectives, take new actions, and garner great results. In law, the definition of a fact is 'the truth about events as opposed to interpretation'.

Many of my clients have become very successful in times of downturn. We all get to choose whether to see the situation we are in as a mess, or as an opportunity. For some people, "the pause" is a very uncomfortable time, so having a tool and structure around big decisions can make all the difference. I hope the Votta Exercise will be the tool that works for you.

But this book isn't just about you. Even though it sets out to assist you in *your* transition, no one exists in a vacuum. The Votta Exercise doesn't just serve the person who practices it. It serves the people with whom that person lives, works, and perhaps even passes on the sidewalk. If you are a leader who wants your team to feel empowered, feel they have a future, to feel heard, and to feel their leadership is transparent, this book is for you. Whether you are in the owner's seat of the company or in a leadership position where you have ownership of the workplace culture, the decisions you make every day make a difference in your team members' lives. This book is for leaders for whom both results *and* people matter.

If that's you, consider this book to be an invitation— it is opening the door for you to be who you want to be and start building a legacy.

Chapter 1

The Votta Exercise Origin Story

> *"Life has no meaning a priori... It is up to you to give it a meaning, and value is nothing but the meaning that you choose."*
>
> – JEAN-PAUL SARTRE, FRENCH PHILOSOPHER

As a business leader, entrepreneur, and/or parent, I'm going to assume you want to take the "right" actions. Conceptually, it's easy to assume that everyone agrees about what "right" means. But the truth is, we all may not agree. In fact, each and every one of us may have a different view on the matter. This is a fact—one that years and years of participating in leadership programs has taught me.

I've been participating in leadership coaching and communication programs since I was ten because my parents were in them, and they wanted me to have as many tools to deal with "life" as possible. As early as middle school, I was saying I wanted to be a psychologist. As a senior in high school, I loved my college-level psychology class; I learned a lot and the teacher made discussing philosophical ideologies or various experiments fun and applicable. In particular, I was drawn to Existentialists, with Kierkegaard, Friedrich Nietzsche, Albert Camus and Jean-Paul Sartre being the most well-known to me.

If you're not familiar with Existentialism, the philosophy is essentially that our lives have no inherent meaning or purpose; rather it is the purpose we create for our lives that gives them a sense of meaning. Once we accept this as a fact, we can live our lives freely, doing what we enjoy, so far as our society allows us. I will write in a later chapter about the definition of *fact*, but Jean-Paul Sartre's quote from *Existentialism is a Humanism*, "there is no reality except in action", turned out to be a guiding principle in my life. And now, it's a guiding principle in my coaching and consulting practice.

As I mentioned, I took a college-level psychology class in high school. One of the things that would have the most profound impact on me was the concept, "correlation does not imply causation." In the late 19th century, British statistician Karl Pearson introduced this powerful idea in math. It became a kind of chant in class; we said it all the time, no matter the philosopher, psychologist, or experiment. *Correlation does not imply causation.* This refers to the inability to legitimately deduce a cause-and-effect relationship between two events or variables solely on the basis of an observed association or correlation between them. When two unrelated things tie together, they can be bound by either causality or correlation.

For instance, we know there is a statistical correlation between eating ice cream and drowning incidents, but ice cream consumption does not cause drowning. In the corporate world, this might look something like believing every time your manager cuts a meeting short, it's because they hate you. Or, it may just mean they enjoy Taco Tuesday, and since you meet on Wednesdays, they have to go the bathroom. Or, they may need to leave at a specific time to pick up their kid from school. Correlation does not mean causation.

Correlation is something we think when we can't see the facts. The less the information we have, the more we are forced to observe correlations. Similarly, the more information we have, the more transparent things become, and the more we are able to see actual causal relationships. In other words, this is an important concept to consider when separating *facts* from *views*. More on that later.

Existentialism really had an impact on me. When I went to college for psychology, however, I learned the majority of undergrad classes consisted solely of learning and regurgitating past methodologies. I understood why, but decided this was no longer my ideal career path.

Although I planned to earn my degree in psychology, I didn't know exactly what career to pursue yet. I enjoyed volunteering in various leadership programs to coach others, and I became a Resident Assistant on campus as soon as I could. I wanted to be a safe person for people to come to, no matter their issue. Although my undergraduate career lasted a few years longer (another story for another book), I continued taking courses to develop my skills in communication, integrity, and accountability. When I left Penn State's Happy Valley, I knew I wanted to help people in some capacity, and coaching seemed like a logical next step.

After college, I worked at three different management consulting firms. When I moved from Pennsylvania to Florida in 2009, I started working with a coach to create the life I wanted. I soon met my husband, Kevin, who introduced me to entrepreneurship, and we started a family. As our kids grew older, I seized the opportunity to lead leadership seminars again—I wanted to share the most important lessons I'd learned through a lifetime of working with, coaching, and consulting others.

The biggest thing I took away from all those experiences was that I could create the life I wanted—everything came down to one's view on a matter. I've applied this concept in my personal life. My kids have nine grandparents, five of them from my side of the family, and four from my husband's side. From a pretty young age, I heard many different versions of stories about the same event, each with its own unique plot, depending on who was telling the story. These stories forced me to take a look at the same situation from different points of view. It wasn't that one version was right and another was wrong. It wasn't that people were lying—which, trust me, took a long time to understand. It was just that everyone had a different view.

I am grateful I had so many communication tools, so much support, and even therapy from a young age that allowed me to discover this critical skill of changing the way we view situations. Sorting through my parents' divorce and remarriage, then a second divorce and remarriage took a lot of work. My kids are now benefiting from the love and support of nine grandparents, and it's nothing short of a miracle. If our family needs help or the kids want to talk to a grandparent, someone is always available. I know I could view this situation differently, but why would I? I choose to view it from a "benefit perspective" on purpose. I believe we all have the ability to shift perspectives—all it takes is a little practice. And you will see it entails more than merely putting a positive spin on what happened.

I have now been coaching people for over sixteen years, and three of those years have been with my business, Votta Coaching and Consulting, now doing business as The Votta Group. My clients come from a wide spectrum of professional backgrounds, from non-profits to the high-level corporate world. Usually, they come to me when they are in the midst of a major transition. They are in "pause" mode, perhaps for the first time in a very long time. This is the perfect moment for introspection. Whether you are in transition because someone put you there or you are creating a transition for yourself, the Votta Exercise—upon which this book is based—provides clarity, power, and access to actions and structures that work for you *right now*.

When picking a name for my company, I started looking at the meanings of my last name. My maiden name is Rink, but it doesn't mean anything cool. (Sorry, Dad.) However, I learned my married name, "Votta" in Icelandic means *to bear witness, to attest, to testify, to certify*. I ran with it. What we take a look at with the Votta Exercise is *what is seen by others.* What is an outsider's view of what is going on? And how does it compare to *our* view of what is going on? There isn't always a "right" and a "wrong." Sometimes, two different views are both "right."

This idea may be controversial in certain workplace cultures. Separating from conventional practices to consider multiple points of view can feel like a risk. Nevertheless, asking questions, such as, *What are the facts about this situation? What are my own views of the situation? What might others see? What is the end result we are all after?* creates the conversation we need to have with ourselves, and with our team.

The Votta Exercise is a tool that seeks to initiate these conversations. I want to make sure it's clear the Votta Exercise in and of itself is a *view*. It is not truth, and it is not fact. It is a six-step exercise to help you decide what actions to take to achieve the results you want in your life and career. No matter how many people achieve great results, those results come from tangible actions. The rest of it is what I put together so you could succeed.

The Votta Exercise is my view on how to help you decide what actions to take to achieve the results you want. My goal was to make an exercise that is easy to use, can be reused, is reliable, and can be scaled to address whatever goal or situation one wants to apply it to. For instance, entrepreneurs can use it to address a specific client relationship, leaders can use it to improve a certain relationship with a team member, or executives can use it to impact their organization's internal culture. The possibilities are endless.

By taking this opportunity to pause and go through the exercise, the steps you need to take in your own life and with your team will become crystal clear. The exercise will also help you become aware of your limiting thoughts and beliefs, freeing you to embark on a journey that makes your vision for your life—your audacious goal—a reality.

I recommend you read this book with a specific goal in mind; otherwise, it stays too conceptual. For example, if you currently have your eyes on a promotion for a specific new role, keep that in mind as you read. Once you grasp the concepts of the exercise, you can go back and repeat the steps with another goal in mind. I want this book to be something you can reference again and again.

As the practice of this exercise will teach you, seeing things from multiple points of view is a superpower no one is born with, but we can always improve, because there is always a different view to consider. There is always something more we can learn from others.

As you read, you will start to create your own view of what the Votta Exercise means to you. And that's what humans do; we take in information and perceive it through the lens of our ideas and experiences. If you want this book to make a difference in your life, it can. I don't want to promise that it *will* make a difference—that is up to you and how you choose to perceive and apply its content. The goal of this book is to give you a tool that supports you through a transition in your life, supports you in leadership, supports your community, and applies to whatever goal you choose.

THE VOTTA EXERCISE
ADJUST YOUR VIEW™

Step One:
Pick a Personal
Goal or Issue

Step Two:
Separate the Facts
from Your View

Step Three:
Choose a View

Step Four:
Look Back

Step Five:
Look Ahead

Step Six:
Reevaluate
(The Bigger Picture)

Chapter 2

Step One:

Pick a Personal Goal or Issue

In Chapter 1, I recommended you read this book with a specific goal in mind. The first step of the Votta Exercise actually requires it. Again, this is a reusable tool, so you can always go back and repeat these steps later with another goal. As we get going, I also want to make it clear this is an exercise, therefore it's something you practice doing. The concepts encompassed in each step aren't complicated, but simply reading about them won't be very impactful.

When picking your goal, you may have a lot of clarity—you know exactly what the goal is and the result you want. But maybe you are still figuring out what goal to choose. Perhaps you are at a crossroads in your career; you aren't exactly sure what the next best step is, or what new service you want to create for your business.

When going through this exercise for the first time, you can't pick an incorrect goal or issue. I do, however, recommend picking something you are dealing with personally, as opposed to an organizational issue. It's easiest to start with an issue that's just for you. Also, pick a goal that can be written down, and someone else could witness. A key part of this exercise involves being able to separate your view (or that of someone else's) from what can be distinguished as fact.

Whatever goal you choose, be specific and make sure it is measurable. For example, if the goal is to offer a new service, how are you going to measure that? Maybe it's by launching a new website with the new service listed by a specific date. That is something someone else can witness, and can easily say that it did or did not happen.

Here's an example of how Paul, one of my clients, came to choose a specific goal to use with the Votta Exercise, and how that goal evolved into another goal. This will help you see the bigger picture and how the exercise plays out in practice.

Paul's Story—Managing People for the First Time

Paul is a highly successful salesperson for a Fortune 500 company. He reached out to me while he was preparing to interview for a promotion. At first, he wasn't sure he wanted the promotion since the new role would require him to manage people for the first time. He felt he wasn't internally prepared to do so. He hired me because although his company had internal leadership development resources, he felt he was missing the training needed to go from being a successful salesperson to a successful manager. Also, with such a transition, he would no longer be working on commission; his success would be tied to completely different measures. *Was he cut out for this? Was this something he was interested in? Was this something he could do well?* He was used to exceeding any and all targets set for him, and taking the time to ask these questions and assess his answers led him to realize he wanted to apply for the promotion.

We spent a lot of time helping Paul consider what this new position would look like: day-to-day interactions with his potential team of colleagues-turned-direct-reports, as well as quarterly meetings when it came to bonus time. He foresaw his view of himself, his team's view of him, and what he thought "should" happen. However, years ago, at a different company, he had gotten feedback about being a "bit of a hothead" and he didn't want that trait to be the reason why he wasn't successful in this new role. I gave him as much space as he needed to share his views and feel heard. It never mattered to me whether he chose to apply for the promotion or not; it needed to be his choice. Once he was sure he wanted the promotion, that became his first goal.

I helped him proactively decide how he wanted to be viewed by others. Of course, we can't control how others view us, but we gain value by asking ourselves questions such as:

- How do I want to be viewed?
- How am I going to view the interviewer?
- What results do I want to create?

The view Paul created of himself was one that was deserving of the position. He had the best results, and he wanted the challenge. I coached him through the various levels of interviews. I asked Paul if he could hand-track as many facts as possible about what the interviewer said. It's a very human phenomenon for our brains to quickly remember our *views* of what happened in a situation, rather than what actually happened. By writing the interviewer's words down in the moment, he and I would have more concrete material to review during our debrief. Post-interview, we used the Votta Exercise to deal with the reality of what happened, and next steps such as who to speak with next and when. We also discussed the view of each conversation, and whether or not the desired result was achieved.

How Human Brains Remember Experiences

It's a very human phenomenon for our brains to quickly remember our *views* of what happened in a situation, rather than what actually happened. Our minds can play tricks on us. In his book, *Subliminal,* renowned Physicist Leonard Mlodinow said, "We basically see what our unconscious wants us to see."

Karim Nader, a neuroscientist at McGill University in Montreal has unconventional ideas within neuroscience. He says it may be impossible for humans or any other animal to bring a memory to mind without altering it in some way. His research has caused some of his colleagues to reconsider their most basic assumptions about how memory works. Nader believes the very act of remembering can change our memories.

Juan Linde Domingo, lead author of a study by the University of Birmingham says, "Memory is a reconstructive process, biased by personal knowledge and world views. We take it for granted that we see the world as it actually is, but in fact, we do not. Our episodic memory, the mind's ability to relive past experiences—we reconfigure it to suit our present needs and world-view."

Memory is closely linked to self-identity, but it is a poor personal record. Each time we relive a memory, we reconfigure it to suit our present needs and world-view. In his book *Pieces of Light*, an exploration of the new science of memory, neuroscientist Charles Fernyhough compares the construction of memory to storytelling. To impose meaning onto our chaotic, complex lives, we need to know which sections to abridge and which details can be ignored. "We are all natural born storytellers. We are constantly editing and remaking our memory stories as our knowledge and emotions change. They may be fictions, but they are our fictions," Fernyhough writes.

So, whenever possible, document facts, conversations, circumstances, and events in the moment, because you may not recall these facts or events accurately. Record a voice memo or write notes down as soon as you can after having a conversation you think was important. Whether it was a tough conversation or you received feedback from someone you respect, you want to remember it accurately.

In the late 1990s, the philosopher David Chalmers coined the term "the extended mind" to describe that when we use pen and paper, calculators, or laptops to help us think or remember, these external objects are incorporated into our cognitive processes. "The technology we use becomes part of our minds, extending our minds, and indeed ourselves into the world," Chalmers said in a 2011 Ted talk.

This is why it was so effective to have Paul write down what the interviewer said, rather than trying to recall events after the fact. It was much easier for me to coach him when he could share what was actually said. Yes, his view of what happened matters. And yes, there are always other ways to look at those same facts (the actual words that were said), so we used this exercise to create next steps that were aligned with what really matters to him.

For Paul, there were many structures to address because the promotion would mean numerous changes in his roles and responsibilities. But we wanted to force that result, which for him was getting the promotion.

I am proud to say that Paul got the position.

Then, he kept using me (and the exercise) to create how he wanted to grow into being a manager for the first time. We started working on a different goal. Paul is a leader where results matter, specifically measurable results, such as revenue and sales targets. But the people also matter, and the way he is viewed by his direct reports matters to him. So, we began using the Votta Exercise to create the way he wanted to manage his team, and the ways he wanted to be seen by his team members. For some of the views he created, there wasn't any witnessable evidence for that view yet, but I assured him we don't need evidence to create the view of ourselves we want. Holding the view alone can be enough to impact reality.

Paul created a view of being trustworthy, knowledgeable, and fun to work with. One challenge he wanted to overcome was the fact that one of his new direct reports had applied for the promotion as well. He didn't want to sweep that situation under the rug; it was something worth discussing to help ensure a great working relationship. Wanting to discuss this with his colleague emphasized the importance of how others view him.

Measuring sales goals is easy—you either meet or exceed the target, or you fall short of it. It is something that other people can witness, because it's a fact. But when it comes to being trustworthy, knowledgeable, and fun to work with, how does one know if they are succeeding with that goal?

Paul found out there wasn't a 360-degree assessment within his organization he could use to gather feedback regarding his soft skills. Paul asked HR if they could help him write and distribute one, but they said their policy was to wait until he'd been in the role for a longer period before such an assessment could be made. Finally, he found a survey on his own and initiated the process himself.

Paul got great, actionable feedback from his direct reports, his superiors, and some of his colleagues. He's now been in the position for about a year. His manager told him he's growing into the role very nicely. Paul took it upon himself to succeed in his new role because, in addition to his sales results, it matters to him how he is viewed as a leader. He continues to use the Votta Exercise to create results. He's always eager to take on what's next in his leadership development, and to also keep developing his team.

***

As Paul's story revealed, one of the first things we did when working through the Votta Exercise together was to reflect upon Paul's own view of himself and the situation he was in, relevant to his chosen goal. To determine his view, however, he had to separate the facts. That brings us to step two.

Chapter 3

Step Two:

Separate the Facts from Your View

After choosing an issue to focus on, the next step is to separate the facts from your view about that issue. The purpose of this step is to determine what is witnessable by others versus what could be going on only in your head—the latter is the part we can control, and therefore it can lead us to achieve our goals.

With regard to the goal or issue you are taking on, take a look at the current state of affairs. If you didn't have to worry about being diplomatic, politically correct, or using the right words, how would you answer the questions below?

- What is currently going on?
- Why is this a problem or goal for you?
- Why are you taking on this problem or goal now?

Some people have a hard time putting their view into words—answering these questions will help determine your current view of the situation. By separating the facts about a situation (that can be witnessed by other people), you'll know that what remains reflects your view.

Here is an example. Let's say you are frustrated because you haven't gotten the promotion you want. You're considering marching into your boss's office and asking for that promotion. You need the higher income it offers to pay for increasing expenses at home, and you're tired of being undervalued.

Let's do some research and consider the facts.

Fact: Your company promoted twenty people two quarters ago, but only promoted one person this quarter.

Fact: Your company laid off zero employees in six months, but laid off over 100 people yesterday.

Fact: Company sales are down significantly this quarter.

Fact: Your current salary is not enough to cover your at-home expenses.

What is left is your view: You're tired of being undervalued.

Given these circumstances, it would make sense not to expect a promotion at this time—the facts show your company is not having a strong quarter. In fact, no one is getting promoted at this time. You not getting the promotion doesn't necessarily have anything to do with you—there is something larger going on with your company. It is, in essence, in a period of "pause."

A lot of people deal with the pressure of needing to be "successful" in their career, no matter what, even when a pause is forced on them. They keep doing what they have always done, viewing the situation with the mindset, "I will *make* this work." Meanwhile, the facts show their bank account contained a certain dollar amount six months ago, and now it has a different, lower dollar amount, revealing that something different needs to be done.

If you are an entrepreneur, feeling unsuccessful, and you are not saying, "When the balance gets to X, that's when I'm going to start looking for job opportunities on LinkedIn," then you are missing an opportunity to control the pause. Or, if you are an out-of-work executive looking for another executive level position, frustrated you are pulling from your 401k multiple times a year instead of accepting a lower-level position to bring in some revenue, you may be missing an opportunity to control the pause.

Again, the amount in your bank account or how many times you pull from your 401k are just facts. Separate these facts, and you can control the pause. Having structures in place—commitments before a crisis happens and emotions run high— clears up a lot of what people worry about, and makes it easier to take actions that produce the results they are looking for. Maybe you *do* need to march into your boss's office, but instead of asking for a promotion or expressing how you feel undervalued, maybe you kindly put in your resignation and ask for a recommendation.

There is always a way to control the pause. Taking the driver's seat makes the biggest difference. It doesn't always go the way we want it to go, but I would say with my own clients, more often than not, it will go the way we want because we have already considered the consequences. When we have already decided what to do next if things don't work out, we are free to take the actions necessary to get what we wanted in the first place.

A Personal Example—Expanding My Business

Several months ago, I decided I wanted to expand my business in Philadelphia, Pennsylvania, where I grew up. This became a goal because I have family in Philadelphia I want to visit more often. As I use the Votta Exercise in this situation, I ask myself: Months later, what are some things other people can witness about this goal? What are the facts?

- If I were to print a report of my business revenue since starting my company, someone could see the billing addresses, for example. There are no addresses in Philadelphia. That is something to which someone else could attest, so I could list it as a fact.
- Someone could take a look at my bank deposits and see there is no income from clients in the Philadelphia region.
- Looking at my credit card statement or my email, there are no invoices to clients in Philadelphia, and

there are no flights scheduled to Philadelphia to visit clients.

These are things other people can see. They're certifiable. Now that I have separated the facts, what is the rest of the story? Why haven't I achieved my goal?

When I take a look at why things are the way they currently are, I can list a lot of reasons why I don't already have clients in Philadelphia. One issue is that when I moved away in 2009, I drank a lot, but people didn't necessarily know. If I were to think about why things are currently the way they are, without any judgment and without being politically correct, I could write these possible views:

- People in Philadelphia don't like me anymore.
- Everyone in Philadelphia found out how much I was drinking.
- The entire city of Philadelphia doesn't want to work with me. (To even write this down or say it out loud seems ridiculously illogical, but it came up as a concern of mine when I wasn't worried about how it sounded.)

I could think of a couple of things that other people could see, other facts about the issue, but the rest of the reasons represent my view of the issue—which is good, because that's what I have the opportunity to work through and change in this exercise.

I could take this a step further and be more specific about my goal. For this example, my goal is to have my first paying client that lives in the Philadelphia area.

I could even say, "My goal is to have my first paying client that lives within fifty miles of the Liberty Bell by the end of this quarter." This is something that someone else could read and say factually, "yes, this happened" or "no, this has not happened."

If I were tracking my notes through steps one and two, I would write:

- **Goal or Issue:** To get my first client within 50 miles of the Liberty Bell in Philadelphia by the end of this quarter.
- **The Facts:** I have no clients on the books with an address in the Philadelphia area; I have no income from clients in that area; I have sent no invoices to clients in that area; I have no flights scheduled to visit clients there; and I have no virtual meetings scheduled with clients based in Philadelphia.
- **My Views:** People in Philadelphia don't like me; people found out how much I was struggling in my past; and no one in the entire metro area wants to work with me.

Let me introduce you to Anna, who, like me, had to separate the facts in order to determine her view.

Anna's Story—Pursuing the Next Promotion

Anna is a female executive working in a mid-size corporation where 95 percent of her colleagues are men. Recently, she was working on advancing her career by pursuing the next promotion. She had even been officially nominated by the leadership team for the promotion.

Anna was having her weekly one-to-one conversation with her manager and heard her say, "*If* you get the promotion..." Anna called me immediately afterwards and talked about her reaction to her manager using the word "*if*". Her view was that use of the word was confirmation her promotion was not really going to happen.

Anna used the Votta Exercise to put her view into words for this situation. Her view was that no matter how much work she did, it didn't matter. A man was going to get the promotion. When reviewing her notes from the conversation with her manager, the good news was there were only a couple of factual bullet points to support her view. The rest of it was *her* view.

Anna was able to shift her view to one that worked better for her. She created the view that she already had the promotion. And, if she already had the promotion, how would she act? How would she interact with others? What actions would she take to support that view?

Regardless of what one's view is, that view dictates the words that come out of their mouth. We will always find evidence for the view we have. Once she adopted her new view, Anna noticed she had a lot more time and energy to put into everything else that mattered to her.

Despite feeling better about her position within the company and the likelihood of getting promoted, after her next weekly check-in with her manager, Anna told me her manager seemed really upset. She told me, "It was the shortest one-to-one we've ever had. I think she was upset with me. I don't think I'm getting this promotion."

We talked about it and separated the facts from her view. Next, just like before, she created a different view and identified actions she would take, given her new view. Less than twenty-four hours later, we found out her boss was leaving the organization in two weeks. Without knowing more—whether her boss was asked to leave or whether she was leaving voluntarily—we had another example of misinterpreting facts. The lesson Anna learned is that we never know why people talk to us the way they do. It may in fact have nothing to do with us.

This is why it can be so valuable to create views that serve us, rather than trap us. I like to use humor with clients. In this situation, I might say, "It was just as likely your manager was abducted by an alien as it was she was talking to you that way because you aren't getting promoted." We might think we have something all figured out, but then we find out a different fact and we learn that our view was way off.

Once we become more adept at using the Votta Exercise, we spend less energy worrying about things for which we have no evidence. We can't control someone else's view, but we *can* make very specific requests about a very specific result, if we do a little bit of work beforehand and reevaluate afterwards. For example, Anna knew when her next conversation with her manager was going to be, and went in ready with a new view of herself and her manager. She paused and got clarity about the specific results she wanted: (a) a yes or no about being promoted—she obviously wanted the answer to be yes, (b) a date for when her manager promised to get back to her, or (c) the name of someone else to contact regarding her promotion. Anna was prepared to make requests and continue the conversation until one of those three requests had been fulfilled.

Working Through Transitions

If you are someone who worries or draws conclusions based on unfounded views—especially when at the crux of a transition—give yourself time to pause and do the Votta Exercise. This is not about a right or wrong way to look at something; it's about being able to look at something from multiple views and picking the one you want.

At some point, a lot of us will have enough evidence that something doesn't work for us and say we are going to look for another job—we're just done. I wish everybody would do this exercise before making a vital decision like this, especially this step: pause and separate the facts from our view of the situation. When we have the view, *"they don't appreciate me here,"* or *"I'm doing everybody's job, but I'm not getting promoted,"* or whatever the view is for you, those views are causing you to conclude it's a good idea to leave. And maybe the views are true, but you will have more clarity once you separate the *facts* from your view.

I have had clients who, just by shifting their view, took different actions, produced different results, and created a completely different experience at the same job. I have also had clients create a different view and maybe leave their jobs sooner because they created specific milestones that made their decision much clearer. Either way, the first step forward after setting a goal is to separate the facts from our views.

This step can be particularly hard for people going through big transitions. I have some clients who are retired military, transitioning from active duty to civilian life. If they seek to start a corporate job, they need to translate what they were good at in military life to corporate terms. Going from active duty, finding a new job, and then learning the new culture of that organization can be a bit of a shock. Sometimes it requires using new words so people can understand what you're saying. Other big transitions occur when people go from corporate America and become an entrepreneur to start their own business, or from corporate America to retirement.

Separating out one's views from the facts that other people could witness may take a little bit longer for people going through these big transitions. In the next chapter, you will release yourself from unfounded beliefs that don't serve you. You'll enjoy letting go of them and exploring new and unfamiliar ways to view your reality.

Chapter 4

Step Three:

Choose a View

Step three forms a big part of the Votta Exercise—it asks you to see a goal, a fact, an issue, or a person from multiple views. As stated in Chapter 1, being able to see things through multiple lenses is a superpower no one is born with, but you can always get better at it. There is always another view from which you can see an issue. Your view is unique to you, given your past and how you are looking at a situation right now. And, it is something you can change on a dime.

Consider the view you uncovered in step two of your goal or issue and ask yourself, "What are some *other* possible views?"

For my ongoing example, one potential view for me is: *Everyone who lives in Philadelphia hates me.* Thankfully that's not a fact; that isn't something someone else could witness or certify.

A second potential view is: *People in Philadelphia have no need for me to coach or consult them.*

A third view could be: *I am not qualified enough to attract clients in Philadelphia.*

A fourth view of my goal could be: *Clients in Phila-delphia have been waiting*. Maybe they have no idea I want to work with clients in Philadelphia, and they are just waiting for me to say, "By the way, I have expanded my market."

A fifth possible view is: *Clients in Philadelphia are dying to give me money*. It's a view, and I hope they're not actually dying. That would be horrible and make it quite difficult for me to coach them!

A sixth view is: *There are clients in Philadelphia who want to give me money.*

Create at least three possible views for the goal you've chosen to take through this exercise. You could create more, if that works for you. Once you are able to start seeing the same issue from multiple points of view, your new skill becomes something that will create a lot of space and power for you.

Now that you've explored many different ways to view your goal or issue, the next step is to *choose one*. Look at the facts from all sides and explore them through different lenses. Which possible view suits you best? Pick one and adopt it as your own. Ask yourself:

- If you could have any view of your goal, or any view of yourself, assuming the goal is accomplished, what do you want to create?
- How would you want to view yourself?
- How would you want to view the goal? Again, this can be anything.

This can be one of the possible views you've thought of so far, or it can be something else. For my example,

I chose, *I deserve to have clients in Philadelphia,* and I like that choice. It matters that you like the new view you choose. When I coach people one-to-one through the exercise, I often get really excited about whatever they created, but that doesn't matter. All that matters is they like the view. My view of, *I deserve this* might not do anything for you. Someone else could look at that view and say, "That's arrogant. I don't want that." Then don't pick that view. You could pick absolutely any view you want, such as, *I am proud of myself,* or *I am successful.*

But again, it needs to be a view. Sometimes participants want to create a view that is action-focused, such as, *I'm going to reach out to people and let them know I'm offering a new service.* That is really great, and it's something others could see. It's a witnessable action and a fact, not a view. A view is something that cannot be immediately witnessed by someone else; it's a mindset from which you then take action.

In my example of wanting to grow my business in the Philadelphia area, the view of *I deserve this* is one that lightens my heart and is just as valid as the previous views I held.

In 2020, there was common agreement among many that, if they were not getting the results they wanted in their careers, it was because of the global challenge at the time: the coronavirus pandemic. I heard comments non-stop, such as, "People aren't buying from me. My business isn't growing because of the lockdown." This is a view a lot of people held onto.

Two clients of mine moved away from that view to ones that served them much better. Meet Gabriel and Vincent.

Gabriel's Story—Making Money Even During a Recession

Gabriel attended my three-hour leadership webinar and realized he was indeed holding onto the common view that people can't make money during a recession. He did the Votta Exercise, and then he was off and running in a different direction.

Gabriel is a consultant whose area of expertise is leadership. He had already done a ton of professional development, but he knew he wanted some guidance during the difficult time of the pandemic. Gabriel had recently moved from a large corporation to a small business, and he was managing people and selling services at the same time. (Most entrepreneurs know this is how it goes sometimes.)

Seeking clarity about time management and new skills to lead others and still be a high performer during times of economic challenge, Gabriel wanted a different view. He wanted to be empowered to succeed, rather than give up and give in to the commonly-held view that success was impossible during the pandemic.

One of the big a-ha's for Gabriel came when he saw he was comparing himself to the former owner, and thought success meant being active in a particular business networking group. He realized he was putting a lot of energy into the one networking group because the former owner had experienced success with them. He thought that in order to have similar success, he had to replicate the former owner's actions. During the exercise, he realized this was not a fact—it was a view. And he didn't even recognize the difference until he got to step three in the exercise.

After creating a different view and wanting to make the biggest difference he could for his clients, having nothing to do with that specific networking group anymore, he realized that was leaving business on the table elsewhere. When he followed up with the other potential clients, he ended up closing more deals than he had in the entire two months prior, just two weeks after doing the Votta Exercise. For him, it was a huge leap toward meeting his newly stated goal. Even though the networking group seemed completely unrelated to the reason why he did the exercise, the exercise helped him make that little shift, which made all the difference. Instead of putting energy into fulfilling a subconscious expectation, he was able to take actions that led to more closed deals. Good job, Gabriel.

Vincent 's Story—Doubling Sales Targets

Vincent is a sales representative for a large national company where revenue is completely paid on commission. He attended the Votta Exercise online workshop when the Covid-19 pandemic just hit, carving out time to learn a new leadership tool. He did a great job throughout the workshop. When I saw him a couple of months later, he was running for a board position for a nonprofit. He thanked me for the workshop and told me he had exceeded his goals for the month. He wasn't sure he was going to hit them, but ended up at 200 percent of his target. He got that board position, too. Vincent is an excellent example of how powerful it is to create your own view in spite of world events.

Common views for people in Vincent's situation may have been, *Nobody is spending money. They're not going to buy from me.* Thankfully, those are just views, not facts. You might ask prospects for sales calls. You might take action and have a great meeting, but they could still say no. And then the next person might say no. And the next person might say no. And then finally, someone says yes.

It's a fact that some people make a profit during challenging times. There are businesses that make money during times of war. There are businesses that grow regardless of, in spite of, or because of global events. It is 100 percent a view to say that nobody is going to buy from you, no matter the situation.

During the exercise, Vincent realized what he had been doing and changed his view. He decided to take the view, *People will see the products I sell will save them money and help them during this economic downturn.* Your actions are very different if you work from that view, versus one that says no one will buy from you. All Vincent did was create a different view about the products and services he sells, and then he followed through by taking actions that had reliably produced results for him in the past, making adjustments to reach potential customers and referral partners virtually. Not stopping and turning the views of the pandemic into a self-fulfilling prophecy made all the difference. To have this view when the entire sales department was saying *nobody is buying right now* was a key differentiator. Vincent now has what I consider to be a superpower.

The key here is to look at a view and recognize it for what it is—a view. Then, once you become proficient in shifting views, you can meet other people where they are and appreciate *their* views. Even if the words coming out of their mouths are the same as other people's, you will start to see that everyone has their own view, and it's rare to have two views that are exactly the same. Having conversations with this ability to shift views will save energy for you, and produce more results with others.

It's not your job to figure out what other people's views are, but as a leader you should appreciate the fact that others have specific views. You should become interested in recognizing their views, and then have conversations to move the needle. The results are so satisfying, and this is how to create a strong corporate culture. You can impact the culture of an organization by taking an interest in other people's views, and keep the conversation about results and actions, rather than arguing about views.

It was easy for Gabriel and Vincent to switch views, take different actions, and get different results. It isn't always this simple or quick, but I want to point out that *it could be*.

Reframing Mistakes

I once stood up a potential new client. I couldn't tell you the last time I stood someone up for a meeting. This is not who I am. And to make matters worse, it was a new acquaintance. I share this example because I can't believe I did it, and I can't deny the fact that it happened.

If we were to do Step 2 of the Votta Exercise, which is to separate what was recordable versus my view of it, I would view the back-and-forth emails to confirm the time. I had offered 9 or 10 a.m. She confirmed 9 a.m., and confirmed the location. This is all in writing. However, on the day of the meeting, I had 10 a.m. in mind.

I messaged her as I was leaving my house at 9:30 a.m. and said, "I might be a couple of minutes late. It might take me a few extra minutes to park and get in there. See you soon!" And she replied, "Great. I have a booth." And I thought, wait! She has a booth already? I realized my mistake: we had scheduled for 9, not 10 a.m. She had been sitting there for a half hour without me, and I was still over thirty minutes away! We rescheduled a meeting for later that day over the phone.

So now, if I were to consider all the different ways to view the situation, my initial reaction was to feel *really bad* about it. I want to apologize, a ton. The perfectionist in me berates me, thinking, *how could I do that? How could I mess this up? This is a really big potential relationship for me.*

But then I thought, what are other views I could take? One is that maybe she loved sitting there by herself for that half hour because she never gets alone time. How about that? Or maybe five years down the road, after she refers my biggest client to me and I help her with a big event she's doing, we get to chuckle about this. That's another view.

I decided I would definitely take the view that this was the beginning of a great new relationship. She'd end up being my friend, and this would be something we look back on and laugh about. If that's the view, when I take action and actually have a conversation with her, I'll say that I'm sorry. I won't over-apologize, however, because then I'm giving her something to deal with. She has to manage my emotions, and it's then her job to make me not feel bad. I'll let her know she does matter to me. Her time matters to me, and I will never do that again. I can promise that. I believe me when I say that. She might not believe me yet, but she will over time, perhaps.

I stood this woman up over a year ago. I'm happy to report I genuinely do consider her a friend. She even surprised me by sending a Bundt cake to say thanks for all of the work I did for her and her organization. I'll never know for sure, but I suspect if I had gone with my default reaction of overreacting and over apologizing, I wouldn't be able to say she is a friend.

I've had people do my workshop, and when they try to figure out what the Votta Exercise is, they label it as positive psychology. "You just need a positive affirmation. Take a negative situation and make it positive." That is not what it is. For a lot of people, when they take a look at the same situation or the same person from multiple views, they do choose something positive. This is great, however, the exercise doesn't stop there. If we don't believe in our new view, our actions won't align with it and we won't have the desired results. To reach that alignment, we may have to look back.

Chapter 5

Step Four:
Look Back

The next step in the Votta Exercise is to pause and notice if there is anything that might hold you back from your new view. If, when you state your new view, any *yeah-buts* come to mind, then it's time to look back.

Once I decided on the view, *I deserve this*, I asked myself if there were any immediate concerns. If I didn't filter my thoughts, were there any potential road-blocks to experiencing the goal this way? For me, with this example, my answer was yes. There were some issues I wanted to take care of before my goal could become reality.

Make a list of any reasons why you think the new view you've chosen can't or won't happen. It can be about yourself. It can be about others. It could be about the goal itself. You don't necessarily have to do anything about this list right now, but it's an important step in this exercise. You can't pretend those things aren't there.

For me, some of my friends in Philadelphia knew how much I was drinking, and some didn't. It's worth saying that my bosses had no idea. There were specific people I needed to have a conversation with if I wanted to build my business "back home". They are the ones I wanted to visit. They are the ones I would want to let know what I was creating. I made a list of action steps that included having conversations with certain friends for the first time in years, conversations with family members, and conversations with past employers.

I moved away from Philly over a decade ago. I don't think it's a coincidence I started working with my coach around the same time as the move. A new environment helped give me a different perspective, and within two months of leaving, I started to see myself differently. I stopped drinking on August 20, 2009. That is a fact. My coach helped me work through unresolved issues in my past, and gave me tangible action steps that helped me much more than I thought they would. As I changed my thinking and my behaviors, I gained momentum to create the life I wanted again.

I had conversations with my family about who I'd been and the things I'd done, and I listened to them when they said they had cried because they were so worried about me. They had probably told me that many times, but I finally heard it for the first time. I could empathize with them and see how much I had hurt them.

I had conversations with two of my friends in Philadelphia about what they thought, knew, or remembered about me from that time. When I had those conversations, I found out my view wasn't the only view. One of them told me she stopped talking to me when I moved because I stopped answering her calls and texts. She said, "You just moved away and stopped communicating with us. So, we didn't know what happened." Oh, I had no idea. Later, someone else said, "Yeah, I missed you a lot." *Hmm*, I thought. *Maybe not all people in Philadelphia hate me.* And some *facts* from when I reached out to some friends and former colleagues: there were still some people who didn't answer when I called, or put off scheduled meetings with me time and time again.

Through this process, something I previously thought unthinkable happened. I was leading a webinar where I shared that I didn't have a single client in Philadelphia and wanted to reach out to that market, when a client participating on the call said, "I met you in Philadelphia." Oh, wow! I didn't realize I *already had* clients from Philadelphia. I hadn't considered that some of my virtual clients could be from Philadelphia. Given my view of *people in Philadelphia hate me*, it didn't even register that I was already coaching people from Philadelphia—people who valued me! I also remembered a wellness client I did accountability coaching with virtually; she was in Philadelphia. There was no space in my old view to see that the goal I was striving for was already a reality in my life—it was a fact that other people could witness.

I want to be clear that step four isn't about therapy. In therapy, you're usually looking for a trigger or some trauma that initiated the trouble you're having.

But when it comes to unpacking the past in this exercise, it isn't important for you to get to the originating event. Looking back is simply the act of making a list of any reasons why your view might not work; if there is anything there for you to take responsibility for or clean up. A clean slate makes a huge difference when you create a plan for moving forward (which is the next step in this exercise).

It is 100 percent up to you to figure out if it is worth taking action on any of those items on your list of why your new view can't or won't happen. Check in with yourself and decide whether or not what happened in your past might hamper your look forward. This is why it's so important to have a goal that is measurable—when you do, you won't have to keep checking in to see if you are accomplishing the goal or not. If you find yourself taking a lot of actions toward your goal but not producing the outcome you want, then maybe you need to do a little cleanup on aisle four. Looking back and addressing what comes up will be worth it. But this, again, is completely optional and unique to your situation. It's up to you.

When I was creating the Votta Exercise, I picked the word "exercise" intentionally, as this is a tool you will practice using. When you use it, it works. No matter how much personal or professional development you have had, no matter the level of corporate training, no matter the level of education or work experience, you are still human. Which means you may see something you thought was a fact is really a view. The good news is that you can always alter a view. No matter how many times you create new views, new actions, structures, and breakthrough results, you can always do it again and again and again. Your view can be malleable; it can change throughout the next week and beyond.

Depending on the next goal you take on, something that is normally easy for you might seem more difficult. For example, seeing things from different points of view might normally come easily for you; maybe it only takes you a few seconds to go through possible different views. With a new goal, though, it might suddenly take you longer to consider something as a view and not the truth.

Give yourself as much leeway as possible to be successful throughout this process. What I mean is, give yourself space to allow for mistakes or upsets as you create evidence for a new view. When you create a new view you have never had of yourself before, and it really matters to you, give yourself grace. When you're looking back and there is a lot to unload, sometimes shifting views can be tough.

It was not easy for me to call people and ask them what they remembered about my drinking in Philadelphia, but I needed to know if I made any messes before I left. I didn't do that with everyone, but it was important for me to create a client base in Philadelphia for personal reasons, and I felt it was worth having some of those difficult conversations. You see, the people I wanted to reach out to and share about my career, catch up, and brainstorm with are the people with whom I wouldn't pretend the past didn't happen. They were my friends and colleagues. The answers I got were not at all what I thought they would be, but I still needed to be open to that process and open to the conversations. If you remain open throughout the process, it will pay off beyond your wildest expectations.

Now, let me introduce you to Allison, who, like me, had to reflect on an unvarnished reality before she could move forward.

Allison's Story—Advancing a Career After 14 Years

Allison, a woman in her late forties, had been working in the same position for over fourteen years. She had been given feedback on an assessment that she needed to be more approachable. She had also been told by other people she had "resting (you-know-what) face." If you are not familiar with this term, it's a facial expression that unintentionally makes a person appear as if they are angry, annoyed, irritated, or contemptuous, particularly when the individual is relaxed, resting, or not expressing any particular emotion.

When you receive similar feedback from multiple sources over time, it's important to seriously examine whether or not it's a fact. Allison was able to see the feedback was given in writing and it was a fact—it was recorded. Whether she actually had this face or it meant she was unapproachable was an opinion, therefore "merely" and luckily a view. Allison was ready to seek the next step in her career, so she wanted to create specific actions and results to receive a completely different kind of feedback.

When we started working on the Votta Exercise together, while explaining the current state of affairs for herself in this area, Allison realized her view was two-fold: first, she thought no one understood what she did, and second, she believed that whatever she did, it wasn't enough.

An increasing number of millennial women had been coming into her organization who smiled effusively and wanted to talk and hang out socially. She unpacked the past and realized that, in her industry a decade ago, she was working primarily with men in the office, and a smile was not needed. What she used to do to get results was no longer working.

Now, given her goal to advance her career, Allison went through the exercise and ended up shifting her view from *I am not approachable* to *I have what it takes, period*. Armed with that new view, she had an unplanned conversation with her partner in the firm and made it very clear she wanted to take her career to the next level. She had not previously shared this so directly. She asked for a plan of steps she needed to take to achieve her goal.

Out of that conversation, she and the partner agreed to change how the organization tracks certain results. This change would impact hundreds of people in her organization. Everyone would be getting credit in a way they didn't previously, all because she had been willing to initiate that conversation.

The fact that Allison had an unplanned conversation and achieved results aligns with the view she created for herself. She has what it takes, period. Even though Allison started out with the goal of moving ahead in her career, she ended up improving the lives of many more people with her actions. She was extremely proud of herself for creating that outcome, as she should be. Brava, Allison!

In the Face of Failure

Sometimes, it can be difficult to face our realities. Our minds so often invent beliefs that aren't real or based on facts, and this goes for both 'positive' and 'negative' views. Some of my clients' first take is very optimistic and positive, but also not "factual". It can have limitations if it's a subconscious choice, as opposed to something you put a little time and focus on. As you complete step four and reflect on your view of a situation, some of these kinds of thoughts from your past might come up. Recognize them for what they are and free yourself from the ways they hold you back. As a leader, it's important to focus on moving the dial forward without letting the past get in your way.

If you find yourself creating the same goal over and over again and not meeting it, step four can really help. Obviously if you're a business owner, revenue and profits matter. If you're fundraising for a nonprofit, money matters. Financial goals always matter.

Let's say your team has consistently failed to meet quarterly goals over and over and over again. But when you are about to create that goal for the 713th time,

I want to make sure you are equipped with the opportunity to look back and re-create their view of that goal. We don't want to create another (or the same) goal on top of not succeeding. Your view of your goal can be incredibly important to your ability to achieve it. It definitely impacts *how* you achieve it, and your assessment of that achievement.

When using the Votta Exercise with your team, people in your company might be excited and raring to move forward at the start; they don't have any thoughts or emotions to manage when they look back. But then there are others who will have a lot to unload from the past; for example, *we have not met this goal for many quarters, and no one is talking about that.* Or they may be worried about bringing others down, or being perceived as something other than a team-player. If you've never allowed your team to look back, then some probably have views you don't want to guide their choices.

This is why we talk about working with senior leaders separately. There is different work with senior leaders. Again, this exercise is for leaders who care about results, but they care about the people almost more than the results. They want employees who are fulfilled, satisfied, loyal, and dedicated, so their clients and customers are also satisfied and will continue to work with them.

When you give your team the opportunity to revise old views, you can start to get real traction when moving forward in steps five and six. What's vital to success is the willingness to work through the hard stuff, if and when it exists.

Chapter 6

Step Five:
Look Ahead

et's take a moment to re-cap each step and how it might play out in the workplace. Let's say you have asked a member of your team to do something three times, but it is yet to be completed. If you were to take yourself through the exercise on this issue, you could lay out the steps you've learned so far in this way:

Step 1
The Goal: Have this employee complete this task by this date.

Step 2
Separate the Facts from Your View
Facts: You have asked this employee to complete this task three times and have given them a deadline, but the employee has still not completed the task.

You didn't give them specific steps on how to complete the task. And they didn't ask.

Views: Maybe you assigned this task as a development opportunity for the employee, based on their earlier behavior as a high-performing employee. You assumed they had time to complete it within the given timeline. Maybe you thought they had a lot of leeway as to how they wanted to achieve the goal, so you didn't lead them through any steps. Maybe you believe they already knew how to deliver on the goal, so you didn't spell out every step they needed to take to achieve it.

Step 3

Choose a View: Take a look at the situation from multiple views. You might lean on your previous experience of when you've asked this employee for help, resulting in the view of *that's just the way they are*. You could use their unresponsiveness in the past to justify what they're doing now. Or maybe you consider what you know about the person's strengths and weaknesses that were revealed in a personality assessment they took with the team.

Maybe they have a lot going on in their personal life. Maybe they are taking care of an elderly parent; maybe they have a sick child, or maybe they are going through a personal crisis. The thing to remember is that you simply don't know what might be causing them to not prioritize your request. You have such a limited view of their reality that for all you know, they could have been abducted by aliens and had a momentary out-of-body experience with no recollection of what they said.

Step 4

Look Back: If there's past frustration, this can be particularly valuable. How many times has this person actually missed a deadline? How many times have you had to follow up with them? Pick the results that matter and look back and see what can be witnessed. What happened? What didn't happen?

Step 5

Look Ahead: This is where we create a plan. Answer the question: *How do you want this issue to play out?* Specifically, how will you measure results?

This step can be done with the employee. I always recommend coming to a meeting with some ideas of what would work. "You can't be late anymore," doesn't work (but if you can acknowledge that end result together, it's a great intention). Think of what can be put in place so this issue isn't talked about anymore.

You may need to work with the employee to figure out a measurable way of recording progress, and what that will look like for both of you in a witnessable way. Separate the facts (things others could observe) from the views as you learned to do in the previous chapters, and create a plan for moving forward.

Let's say the employee picked a view of being a reliable resource for the company. Step 4 can include how many times (in real numbers) the person missed a deadline over the previous three months. Step 5 can be created together with the direct report and include witnessable actions, such as how many deadlines are allowed to be missed in the next three months. As an example, it could be two or less.

Another measurable action could be the direct report reaching out to the manager *before* the manager follows up with them. For instance, they could schedule check in times on Mondays and Wednesdays at 4:00 pm to ensure deadlines are met. It would establish that this initiative isn't just a nice idea.

How to Create a Plan

If you have discussed your goal with others in your life, chances are you have heard everyone else's "best ideas" on how to approach your goal and make it a reality. However, all that matters is that you create a plan that works for *you*, looking ahead and moving forward.

As part of creating a plan, there are certain structures and actions that need to be put in place for your new view of yourself and your goal to become reality. What do you need to do to make that happen?

Here are a few examples of structures you can put in place to make progress toward your goal:

- Schedule and conduct interviews with subject-matter experts.
- Research what has already been done, or what is already known about a topic.
- Shadow someone for a day who already succeeds in the area.

- Create a timeline with weekly objectives to track your progress and success.
- Define risks and decide how you will mitigate them.
- Block out dedicated time on your calendar to ensure these structures support the progress you want to see.

There were times when I had to have someone on the phone with me in order to hit send on an email. It wasn't because I didn't want to send the email, and it wasn't because I didn't want the client—it was simply because I hadn't sent the email. One time I had someone reach out to me and ask for a proposal. It was an ideal client, and they followed up with me twenty-four hours later, asking, "Hey, how are you? I look forward to getting your proposal." For whatever reason, another twenty-four hours passed. I finally asked another consultant for help, saying, "Hi, even if you're working on something else, let's stay on the phone. I'm not hanging up until I hit 'send'."

I don't know why I needed that level of support at that time. I don't know why I avoided sending the proposal. I also don't care. I needed to hit send and get the proposal out because this client wanted to work with me, and that's what it took to get it done.

What will it take to make your goal happen? Maybe you have to corner yourself in. No one wiggles out of commitments more than I do, especially the ones I've made to myself. What's important is figuring out how to set up your life to achieve the success you're after.

Put structures in place so you are accountable to your goal or view. Maybe you are a high performer, and the thought of adding more blocks of time on your already-full calendar makes your skin crawl. I've had clients who, after taking a look at a goal or an issue, realized all they needed to do to create a different result was to create a different view. They were good to go and pleasantly surprised by their results.

If you find you have more work to do beyond creating a different view, set up the structures for progress, especially when the view itself is personal to you. There are multiple ways to achieve the results you want, and multiple ways to fulfill your goals.

The first time you make a list of everything you want to do, I recommend doing a brain dump of every possible action you could take to achieve your goal. Ask yourself if there are structures you can put in place to almost "force success" to happen.

Forcing Success

My clients often ask how to *force* the success they want. The first step is to get clarity on what success looks like.

Perhaps you have a goal that is traditionally difficult to measure, such as being fulfilled, or inclusion. You'll need to turn those into measurable goals. I believe you can set up structures around intangible goals. How would you measure a sense of fulfillment or inclusion as a leader? Or, how does your organization currently measure those things?

Once those measures are in place, the next step is to get clarity on how you will get results or move the needle in that area. Learning about yourself and the ways you might prefer to work is also helpful at this stage. For instance, I have some clients who are very deadline-oriented, while others prefer to get something done as soon as the task or goal is on their plate. It doesn't necessarily matter how you have gotten things done in the past—we want to nurture your strengths, give you more choices, and more ways to achieve the success you want.

If you are taking on something new and it's not going the way you want, it's not that there is something wrong with you. Sometimes people think they need to stop being a certain way. For example, they have received feedback they are too direct when they speak, so they think they have to change that about themselves. No, keep that trait, and use the Votta Exercise to get better at being how you want in conversations. It also doesn't mean you should drop the goal; there just might be ways to corner yourself in to get the result you want. When you are planning for a certain result, how you plan to get that result, no matter what, is different for everyone.

I also work with leaders who want their teams to have these tools so they can reliably produce results in ways they hadn't before. When I say, "force a success" or "force a certain result", it may sound a little dramatic, but it just means you get to be in charge of your results, rather than leaving them to chance.

It's worth putting in time on the front end as a leader so you are able to achieve new results, achieve them in new ways, surprise yourself, and then enjoy those moments. If it matters to you to be proud, and it matters for your team members to be proud of themselves and the results they produce, this exercise is a great way to make that happen.

Below are some possible structures to consider.

Structures with Personality Assessments

There are so many assessments out there about personality profiles and how to communicate with different types of people. When you lead others, you must allow them to grow and change, just like you do. I've seen a lot of leaders produce impressive results with their teams or organizations when they are open-minded and create structures to remind themselves and their teams that growth can happen at any time.

When it comes to personality tests, I understand they have a place. In my opinion, they can be effectively used to streamline the hiring process. However, I always recommend for people to take them with a grain of salt. Since your staff's training and development matters to you, I would be careful not to relate to people as if they were in a box. Personality isn't static, nor is it all-inclusive. An introvert can be very good with people, for example.

Regardless of your opinion about personality tests, it's worth researching the assessments and adjusting the findings to match your culture. Meaning if growth and development are valued by your organization, make sure you give your employees language to align with those values.

You want your team to be able to excel in any area they choose. As a leader, it matters to me that I acknowledge the successes of the people around me. The Votta Exercise allows for the kinds of conversations where if somebody says they want to be good at something, they can—they simply adopt that view, put structures in place, and then make it happen. To do this "simply" may or may not be "easy," but the exercise is available for reuse at any milestone or bump in the road.

When I coach someone through the Votta Exercise, I want them to flourish, grow, have tools, and be empowered in the ways they want to be empowered. The steps make sure you're not skipping anything; when you don't ignore any of the steps, the exercise really does allow for growth in unprecedented ways.

Feedback Structures

Whether you're getting feedback from a client or a boss face-to-face, emailed in advance, or multiple people give you feedback at the same time, you can use this exercise to plan how you view that feedback, how you respond to it, and how that feedback will impact your results afterwards.

Even structures for receiving feedback can be changed. I intentionally include that I will ask for feedback at least twice during my six-month-contracts with executive coaching clients. I don't want to wait until there's a problem to ask how things are going and have measurable results. By asking for feedback, I can measure not only my success but theirs, also, and check in to see if we should change how they want to measure their success.

Giving feedback can be hard. If it's an official evaluation, then you have a formal structure and an understanding of the Key Performance Indicators (KPI) that are being measured. You may have to deliver difficult feedback because there is a gap somewhere, something the client needs to work on, or something just isn't working. Doing the Vottta exercise to intentionally create a productive and positive experience during the conversation can help with delivering that feedback. Ask the following questions:

- How do you want to view them?
- How would you like for them to view themselves?
- How would you like for them to view you?

Your views can all be created prior to going into the conversation. This may be one of those times when you might not think it's useful to do an exercise like this, but it can create a huge impact, and it's not just about the results for you—it's also about the people. Implementing this exercise is one way to have the people around you grow, and grow continually, because you aren't keeping them in a certain box.

Maya's Story—Creating a Legacy

As my executive coaching clients practice the Votta Exercise with me and surprise themselves by achieving new results in new ways, they naturally want to become leaders who teach their teams how to benefit from adjusting their view, as well.

I'm working with Maya, a female executive for a hospital in Philadelphia. She says that after learning the Votta Exercise, she feels joy in her career for the first time in over a decade. She has already let the CEO know (in front of all the hospital senior leadership) that she is ready for more responsibility. Now, she is working on accepting feedback (referring to the literal words in emails, cards, and what's spoken to her), and therefore accepting her successes... because she views it that way! Maya plans to bring me in to conduct workshops with the directors and use the Votta Exercise to empower them in their leadership, culture, and improve various specific results. Simultaneously, she understands the feedback she gives to her team can make a big impact. Maya has created new timelines for giving feedback to her team, with new "views" for each person. She created gaps in their leadership for them to grow into, and detailed development plans with actions as to how they can do that. Maya wants to create a legacy and make the hospital better because she was there to make a positive, lasting difference.

Structures to Measure Views

If you choose a goal that is measurable (i.e., earn $25k more next quarter) it's easy to track. But what about tracking your progress with new views? That seems more intangible.

There are a lot of soft skills that seem immeasurable, like feeling fulfilled or being inclusive. They can seem subjective and stay that way. I'm here to tell you that those are the kinds of things we want to make measurable as well. Then, we set up a plan, take action, and make it happen using the Votta Exercise. In my personal example from earlier, if I just think in my head that I'm maintaining my new view, *I deserve this*, then that too, is just a view. So, how can I measure if I really am maintaining this new view? What structure could I put in place to make it more of a fact?

One structure I could put in place is to carry around a sticky note or small notepad. Every time I catch myself thinking *I deserve this* (my new view), I can make a little tic on the paper. At the end of the day, I can count up the marks and prove to myself and others that I am maintaining my new view. On the days when I only have a few marks, I'll know I need to see if there are any correlations. For example, I realized that if I have a deadline for work, or if we are running late for school and I could be late for a coaching call, I'm more likely to yell at my kids. If I didn't track that, I might not have noticed. Does correlation mean causation?! *Still no.* But I was able to adjust my view, and create a new structure that worked. I stopped scheduling calls at 9am, and I now wake up earlier on the days when we need more buffer time. This keeps my view aligned with the progress I am making toward my goal. It makes the seemingly immeasurable become measurable.

The Votta Exercise can help you measure the things that seem immeasurable. Satisfaction at work can be measured, and it looks different for you than for other people. What is important is to have an introspective conversation about what satisfaction looks like to you versus others, and to put in place a structure to achieve it.

There are multiple creative ways in which structure can be created. Here is an example of structures that worked for my client, Maria.

Maria's Story—Intentional Downsizing

Maria is an entrepreneur who, after doing the Votta Exercise for the first time, created the result of intentional downsizing. She realized the way certain clients interacted with her wasn't working, so she created new structures and decided she wouldn't renew those client contracts.

One of the structures she implemented were monthly check-ins. That way, she didn't have to wait for something to go wrong before responding to a situation. She knew exactly what she was accountable for, what she had and hadn't done to date, and exactly what she was doing if she went above and beyond what the contract stipulated.

The check-ins helped Maria so much when meeting with her clients. Before she created a plan, she used to go into meetings thinking she was in trouble, which felt horrible. But when she took the time to review exactly where she stood on her obligations, she could feel confident and much more relaxed when meeting with clients because there were no surprises. She could easily point out where she was going above and beyond expectations.

Another part of her monthly check-ins involved her own internal feelings about each engagement. Because she had all those feelings swimming around in her body, she was losing sleep. To help make her feelings more tangible and even measurable, I created a survey to help her understand what was going on. We made the seemingly immeasurable measurable, simply by ranking these factors on a scale of one to five. The practice consisted of getting her feelings out of her head and written on paper. If she found that month after month she marked "one" with a client, she simply wouldn't renew the contract with them the next time it came due. If she found herself at a four or five with a client most of the time, then she knew she wanted to continue doing business with them.

Maria and I recently worked together again and used the Votta Exercise after she accomplished her initial goals. Again, the exercise is something people can reuse as circumstances change, and as what matters to them changes. Maria is very proud of the life she has created, and right now she has clients who are causing her to lose sleep for the first time ever. This is not something she wants. This time, when we did the Votta Exercise, she recognized she had the following view: *she was in trouble with multiple clients at the same time.*

Step 1 of the exercise, where we separate the facts from the view, was eye-opening for her. When she looked at what other people could witness compared to her view, she realized that most of what she thought was true was *coming from her view.* This was an invaluable exercise for her. This may seem like a simple concept, but when it comes to the things that matter in our lives, we tend to be myopic or subjective. It doesn't matter how many times I do the exercise myself—when it's in an area that really matters to me, there's always a fact that, to my surprise, I discover is only a view. How lucky is that?

For Maria to look ahead, she set up a structure to separate facts from her views of those facts. Her new view is that she is happy and relaxed. Sleeping through the night matters to her because it is a large contributor to feeling happy and relaxed, and is something that can be witnessed and tracked.

Another structure Maria set up was to have a notebook by her bed. If she wakes up in the middle of the night and needs to write things down to get them out of her head, she does that. First thing in the morning, she reviews a list of her current clients. If out of the seven companies she's working with, she thinks she's in hot water with three of them, she picks one of those companies and calls that president. This structure is set up to create evidence for the view she's created.

She also sits down weekly and reviews all her client projects, assessing current and potential problems. Included in the structure is the fact that at some point, she may not need to do this weekly anymore, or eventually not at all. She recognizes what we call "happy red flags."

A happy red flag is being able to figure out what a situation looks like to someone else. What can someone else witness when she feels like she is in trouble? For example, her husband can see she is not sleeping. Or, if she wears a watch that can track her sleep patterns, it will show her exactly how much sleep she got the night before.

Another happy red flag built into her structure is if she spends two hours wasting time scrolling on the internet, instead of getting work done. For someone else, spending two hours on social media might not be a red flag, but for Maria, it's evidence she is in trouble. If somebody else knew she was scrolling on the internet instead of working, it would be a problem. She knows that mindlessly scrolling online is something she does to cope when she is avoiding something.

According to her structure, these actions are measurable evidence that she is in trouble. These red flags point to her view that she is in trouble, but they are *happy* red flags, because she *wants* to find them. The red flags help her track her behavior so she can better achieve the results she wants.

Chapter 7

Step Six:

Reevaluate (The Bigger Picture)

The Votta Exercise can be used to regularly reevaluate what is important to you or determine the next step in your career. As scalable as this tool is, you can use the exercise to reevaluate each step of the exercise itself.

Let's say your goal is to figure out the next step in your career. You even tie a date to your goal. You have no idea how it's going to look or what's going to happen, but you give yourself until the end of the quarter to get clarity about that next step. Some people get a lot of value from stopping at step three in the exercise and reevaluating what really matters to them. They realize they could view themselves in any way, and it doesn't matter if they have evidence for that view yet. They start to inject their new view into their lives, and evaluate what changes in their lives as a result.

One of the biggest opportunities provided by this exercise is that it can be used to evaluate a specific conversation with a specific person at a specific time. You can use the exercise to force the success you want from a specific conversation. You can also use it to reevaluate your whole career. When a close family member gets sick, there is a death in the family, a divorce, or a layoff—these are the times when we often reevaluate what's important, because unexpected circumstances are thrown our way. What I recommend to leaders reading this book and to my clients is to schedule time to reevaluate when life circumstances call for it.

For example, many of my clients intentionally sit down and schedule time to fill their client pipeline or focus on sales. Or, they schedule time with me, attend a webinar, bring me in to consult and coach with managers, or go away for a weekend and do the work to reevaluate. The end result could be the same circumstances they are already in, but being in the driver's seat, being empowered, and having the choice to view things however they wish is a powerful tool.

Some leaders even take on the view that they want their employees to choose to stay with their company over and over again. They give their team members an opportunity to answer the question, "If you could create anything, what would you want to create?" Or they ask, "If you could look at yourself any way, how would you want to see yourself? If you could see your results here at work, what would you want to be known for?" To give people that kind of freedom and choice can be scary for a leader sometimes. What if they choose to leave the company and you lose the best people you have?

It's up to you to determine your end goal, depending on your view and how empowered you want your team members to be. How do you want to create your culture? How will you make it real? This is why I say the exercise is scalable. This is something you and other leaders in your company can get used to, using it to empower your employees and allowing them to adjust their view of themselves and their results. Leaders are sure to see the impact on the bottom line, but also the impact on the people.

Amber's Story—Creating New Services

Amber is an entrepreneur who first learned the Votta Exercise in a workshop and began working with me one-on-one roughly a year later. She wanted a boost in creating a new service, and wanted to create it intentionally and reliably. She wasn't sure whether she would create a new company or not, but she did end up creating a completely new arm of her business and wanted it to take off.

Creating the actions and structures was exciting for Amber. There was very little shifting of view needed. It was more about putting her new service offerings into words and then going for it. Since it was a new service, she didn't need to do Step 4. For Step 5, look ahead, she came to our calls with plans and timelines already in place.

But then something changed. Weeks would pass before we had another conversation. She had missed enough deadlines and had to admit to herself we needed to reassess. None of the dates worked anymore. The structure that was sufficient two weeks ago was no longer working. So, now what?

One of the great things about Amber is that she already knew there was nothing innately wrong with adjusting her view. We are able to do that at any time. Amber could see there was nothing wrong with her, and she was quickly able to do steps 1 through 5, putting new actions and structures in place to have the launch happen as planned.

However, when it came time to measure and reevaluate her success, Amber knew our previous structure of weekly check-ins made it too easy for her to miss some of the important deadlines she had set. She went back through the exercise quickly, and we set up a new accountability structure. She started sending me multiple text messages throughout the day to help motivate her to stick to the plan, and not let everyday firefighting pull her off task.

One of the things she set up from the beginning were registration goals. For example, Amber said if she didn't have a certain number of participants by a certain date, she would offer a partial scholarship. For her, this goal was not coming from the view that there was something wrong, or from a sense of scarcity. It came from an intentionality about how many people she wanted in the program. This wouldn't work for everyone, but worked for her at that time, given the view she chose for the goal.

In the end, she didn't need to use the partial scholarship. She exceeded her registration goals, which was phenomenal. However, when it came time for content creation, she missed a couple of deadlines again. She saved energy by not blaming herself, and instead spent her focus and energy wisely by looking ahead. Amber had an open conversation with herself about missed deadlines and what she would do to get back on track. She asked for support because it mattered to her that she felt safe to do the work going forward.

Amber created a new timeline and texted me when it was done. The structures she set up were very detailed. One view might be that she was micro-managing the situation. From the outside, someone might have thought it was crazy to send so many texts as she finished small tasks. But she did this because it was easy for her to create more structure— the result mattered.

She was able to use this structure as an example with her employees. She was intentionally creating her company's culture and using it as an opportunity to show them it's not okay to miss a deadline, but it is okay to need help and add structures to make sure deadlines are met. She told them it's okay to say, "If by this time I don't have that done, everything else stops, and we do that." Obviously, there is an impact on everyone when that happens. We don't want that to happen, but structures are intentionally set up so that either way, the client wins and the team has a sense of success. They set up a post-mortem after each engagement to evaluate what worked, what didn't work, and what they would shift going forward.

For Amber, it wasn't just the result that mattered. The people also mattered, and she found a way to combine those two factors very successfully.

Vision and Mission

As already stated, the Votta Exercise is scalable, and can be done as a group. There are many times I've gone inside an organization and everybody knows what the goal is. The company states the vision, mission, and values. They even have those guiding principles prominently posted somewhere visible. However, if the vision or mission are not producing the desired results, it may be time to reevaluate.

The exercise itself can be used to create your company's mission and values, whether done individually or collaboratively. If working in a group, you could have the goal of the exercise to be the creation of your mission and values by the end of the meeting, or by noon today. Then, you can create a view of that goal together.

When working through the exercise, some people might have a lot of baggage to deal with if they have been working in their industry a long time. Or, they might not have anything to deal with at all. For some people, this might be the umpteenth time they are creating the mission and values for a company. For others, this might be the first time they are being included in the process, and they don't have anything to look back on. Either way, it's worthwhile to work through the steps together with the intention of completing the group goal, which for this example, would mean having your mission and values written out and agreed upon. Then, all you have to do is make sure they are dispersed as needed.

The Opportunity of Leadership Retreats

In another example of using the Votta Exercise within an organization, I once led a board retreat for a non-profit. It was the first time the board of directors, the junior board of directors, and all of the managers had a meeting together.

When dealing with a group, you can't assume that everyone is fully on board with the goal or the mission. As I have already stated, no two views will ever be the same, and the leaders who practice the Votta Exercise care about the things that matter to their teams.

The nonprofit already had a mission and created a very specific goal regarding new revenue from their fundraising efforts. When we looked at possible views for the fundraising goal, I coached the leaders to watch who was speaking, and how they were speaking. For example, were a lot of people interacting? It mattered to leadership that people felt heard, and that the effort was collaborative. This was why they had brought me in. These insights were invaluable for these leaders, because we were able to coach from what actually happened in the retreat.

In Step 3, they created a view that the process was going to be easy; that money coming in would make it possible for them to make the difference in their community. When unpacking the past, it took a while for people to begin sharing their concerns. It's one thing to do that kind of work individually, but it takes guts to tell the truth out loud about a particular topic, issue, person, or circumstance, especially in a room full of people we may or may not feel safe sharing information with. The retreat was very telling, and we left having fulfilled the intention of creating actions and structures necessary to achieve their fundraising goal.

As part of Step 5, we had a new goal, we had a plan, and some specific actions that people promised to take. And as a part of the structure going forward, we set up individual coaching with the CEO of the organization and the President of the Board of Directors. No one wanted this to be another training they attended only to put a booklet on their shelf and never revisit it again.

This was perfect since the exercise is designed to create sustainable, breakthrough results. The CEO and I noticed there had been a large percentage of people that didn't contribute during the meeting, even when they were called on. Either they didn't have any ideas, or they didn't want to say anything. This was something they wanted to change.

There were also employees who had not been in the room since the retreat was only for the management team, the board, and the junior board. So, they created an anonymous staff survey. They decided that they'd rate employee satisfaction every quarter. They had never done this before, and in that first round of surveys, only about 50 percent of the people filled them out. They wanted 100 percent, but for a first-time survey, I suggested to shift their view: 50 percent was a really great outcome for this first step in creating a transparent, supportive culture.

It was important for their employees to be aware the survey was coming every quarter. They felt that maybe their staff needed to shift their view or to trust that, first and foremost, it really was anonymous. Second, employees needed to trust that their responses would be used for good. (And let me tell you, if you ask people what's right and what is good, you will see many different answers. There is no clear answer for what "*good*" is.)

What really impressed me about the leadership is they wanted to hear from people, and they wanted to make the changes that were suggested. Since the retreat, there have been big transitions in their organization. For example, the second-in-command is now first-in-command. It was a sudden change, and if you were to ask the board of directors, it was a tough decision. But the way the transitions have been handled, from internal communication with employees to external communications with referral partners and the community, has been inspiring to watch. My view is that this organization has been using the tools and reaping exceptional benefits.

A Note on Equity, Equality, Diversity, and Inclusion

Many of my clients have been pioneers for gender parity and equity in the workplace. Many have used the Votta Exercise to support their commitment to creating an inclusive culture.

Equity, equality, diversity, and inclusion come up when leaders are creating a culture from scratch, working for a corporation that already values diversity and inclusion, or dealing with issues that are less tangible, but negatively impact the workplace culture. In the case of the latter, existing actions and structures aren't sufficient, or aren't getting the desired results.

One way to approach these challenges, just like with any other value, is to do the exercise with a group of people. I always recommend having a third-party facilitate this type of event. That way the meeting environment will be safe, straightforward, and a place where people can be vulnerable and honest when assessing their own leadership.

While I am not an expert in diversity and inclusion, one thing I'm very good at is creating an environment where people feel comfortable. Therefore, when I facilitate, leaders in the organization can look at things they would normally sweep under the rug and wish would disappear. Because equity and inclusion can be such a difficult topic to discuss, having this conversation is crucial.

Some organizations go to all the trouble of setting up diversity and inclusion programs for the sake of checking a box. They end up with some nice words on their website, but with Glassdoor and other sites that rate employers, the illusion won't persist. When you care for your company, you must care for its employees. Giving people a safe space to examine their thoughts, opinions, generalizations, and biases can make a difference when it comes to retaining valuable talent. You lead, and they will follow your lead, so what you do matters.

A 2018 report issued by McKinsey Global Institute titled "Delivering through Diversity" makes a valuable assessment of how the social issue of diversity and inclusion plays out in businesses today. Their conclusion was that it's no longer a matter of social justice or legal compliance, but gender diversity and inclusion (GDI) represents a distinct advantage for modern-day organizations. In fact, a study conducted on over 1,000 companies in twelve countries found a clear correlation between "diversity in the leadership of large companies and financial outperformance."

McKinsey also found the following:

- Diversity and business performance are positively correlated.
- Leadership matters.
- Gender is only the tip of the iceberg (i.e. inclusion is also important).
- Failure to change is costly.

The beauty of inclusion and of the Votta Exercise is they put you in a constant state of curiosity. It's not about putting people in certain boxes or stereotypes. It's about the desire to hear other points of view. It's about having curiosity about people and the talent they bring to the organization. It's about hiring staff that offer a wider range of skills, and creating more innovation when it comes to generating revenue, decreasing costs, and creating the culture you want.

By having this exercise facilitated by a third party, people will feel that they matter, and they are heard. They will feel that leaders are transparent, and they are safe. It might take a little time for people to start acting accordingly, as building trust takes time. I have worked with organizations that had already created an environment of trust, and people opened up immediately. But sometimes the trust isn't there, and people are skeptical. When my experience in leading groups makes me feel like people are holding back, I work with top leaders after the workshop, and we plan another workshop for a different topic or goal. The more times we do the exercise, the more people start to trust the process, the leaders, and the organization.

Some leaders think the only measurable factor of diversity and inclusion is the number of employees they have from each race or ethnicity. But that's far from true. When working step 5, get creative about your structures and how you can measure against them.

Ask yourself, *What does it look like for people to be committed to inclusion in your organization? What do* they *say it looks like?* Whether you do this exercise in one-on-one conversations or in a group setting, you will be able to get more clarity and buy-in, and come up with more structures you can measure. Then, with these clear expectations and consequences in place, it will be much easier to hold people accountable for achieving and maintaining an equitable, inclusive culture.

My clients know how important this is, and many are trailblazers in this area. Where the Votta Exercise helps is when a corporation is doing their 973rd Diversity, Equity, and Inclusion (DEI) training, and the people—especially upper management—aren't really doing the work because of their view. It could be because they think they already have it handled, it's not their problem, etc. However, when working with me, people feel safe to examine without judgement, and have had big breakthroughs. They are then able to share that vulnerability and create their desired culture. Do the work to figure out what being inclusive looks like (witnessable) in your organization, and yes, you receive all the benefits of attracting top talent because of the strength in diversity.

When creating what inclusion looks like for your organization, it can be a collaborative effort. It's sometimes valuable to separate the most senior leaders to do some deeper LOOKING BACK before rolling out initiatives throughout the organization. Understanding how employees VIEW themselves, and having clarity on the actions that work and don't work are vital to creating an inclusive culture.

Reassessing Employee Recruitment and Retention

When it comes to hiring or firing someone, I've seen leaders repeatedly decide to let go of a team member, or perhaps not even hire them, because they didn't hit the target matrix of a personality assessment or company measurement of success. Often, the candidate they let go of joins a competitor's company and becomes an extremely high performer.

As a leader, your view of the employee or candidate can make the difference. Case in point, I recently spoke with a friend who owns a business with about 80 employees while she was in the process of hiring. She had decided a particular candidate was not a good fit for the culture. I began asking her why, in order to separate the facts and determine her view. Once I got a little bit more information, I suggested a couple of other views she could adopt about the candidate. For example, he would be very motivated because of X, Y, and Z.

I found out she actually ended up hiring this person, and he's brought in some of the company's largest accounts over the last six months. Our brains are so frequently making decisions for us, treating views as if they are facts, and turning those views into actions. Knowing when to create a pause and do the work of the Votta Exercise is a superpower. The exercise can make such an impact on the bottom line, your day-to-day life, and your career that I recommend doing it before making any big decision about hiring, firing, quitting, or accepting a position.

Measuring your own success and that of your employees, using measurements that everyone understands can make it easier for you as a leader when it comes to making difficult decisions. Ultimately, we want to retain the talent we have. I know the amount of time, money, and energy that goes into training and finding great people.

Too many small business owners hire people based on gut feeling alone. They decide whether or not a person is a fit for their culture based on an opinion or view, rather than putting measures in place to help determine if that person is a good fit. By using a measurable tool, the process occurs outside of you—it is no longer about you.

If you want a certain percentage retention of your clients, or a certain percentage retention of your employees, evaluate how it's going and decide if something needs to shift—whether it be your goal, your view, or how you measure success. Organizations often bring me in for consulting on this topic because reevaluating these structures can have a strong impact on the bottom line.

Using Transitions to Pause and Reevaluate

Transitions happen in life. Again, sometimes it feels like they happen to us, and other times we choose them as an option. Either way, it's like having children. Whether you're ready for parenthood or not, at a certain point, the baby arrives and you have to adapt.

In March 2020, when the government began implementing quarantine restrictions in an initial attempt to curb the Covid-19 pandemic, the business my husband owned could not open its doors. Given the nature of the service he provided, he could not operate virtually. Our household income was impacted by this, as he was the higher earner.

Each of us reacted to the situation in our own way. We did the Votta Exercise together. We wanted to get to reality quickly to see how we would actually be affected. The facts that could be witnessed were: 1) the dollar amount in our business checking account, and 2) the latest news reporting the date the government stated businesses would reopen. Even if the news changed rapidly from one hour to the next, it was still recordable evidence.

Gathering the facts, even with the understanding they were changing quickly, was not easy, and it wasn't always fun. There was, however, a comfort in being able to control my view of an uncontrollable situation. We just decided to be okay with whatever our initial reaction was, and to recognize that it stemmed from our view. Our initial reaction to a change is based on a view we have not put into words yet.

Before we could put words to a possible view of these facts, we had to ask what our goal was. We had a very specific income that Kevin had reliably brought into our family household, and that was being impacted. When we were ready, we worked together with our coach and listed all the ways we could view what was happening. We wanted to see this as an opportunity because we had created a partnership for revenue in our household, as we are both entre-preneurs. I had a promised dollar amount from my business that I contributed to the household, and he did, too, but it wasn't going to happen for a while. Our situation had changed.

To view this as an opportunity going forward, there were some things that came up when we looked back. I had made promises in the past that I hadn't fulfilled, so we talked about that. My husband also had a view of himself as a provider. He had to make a dramatic shift and adjust his view quickly, and from there we created a whole new action plan with whole new structures, and whole new numbers.

I could not be prouder of what came from the work we did. I felt completely supported by my husband. I am incredibly thankful for the growth of my business. I have the view that if my business grows, I'm helping other people create jobs. I'm helping other people grow. I'm helping other people, period. That's my view of what I do. I empower people to love what they do.

This is an example of a time when a transition was put into our laps. We did not choose this, and as a result, it has pushed us in a direction that I don't know we would have gone otherwise. As it turns out, it has really worked to our benefit. I love working. My husband loves being with our little kids, and now he is with them more often than ever. Now we have more time to do the things we love. This time has forced us to get clarity on what we want, and then set up structures to make these things happen. In other words, it forced success.

A global pandemic made us reevaluate. Many of the people I work with set up structures to force this kind of introspection without a traumatic event. People are choosing to stay at a job that pays them very well, where they have been successful. Or, they are leaving to start their own company or find another job. Those kinds of transitions are difficult. There are transitions you are going to choose. Given your view, the transition either makes sense, or it doesn't. Choose one option, or the other. If by adjusting your view, that transition no longer looks like a good idea, it's worth pausing and doing this exercise before taking any further action. If you are able to shift your view and it completely alters the trajectory, why not take the time to be in the driver's seat completely? Control the pause, and then create actions and structures that are in line with what you really want.

Chapter 8

Coaching Others through the Exercise

As you gain experience with the Votta Exercise and see it start to produce positive results in your own life and career, you may wish to share it with others, whether it be family, friends, or members of your team. This chapter shares some tips and tricks about what to expect when you facilitate the Votta Exercise with others.

Don't Give Advice

Maybe you've had this experience when working through the exercise yourself—you see something from a different view and share it with somebody, and they say, "Duh." Or they might say, "Of course, you should have fired that person a long time ago." Once, as I was facilitating a group and shared a personal example from within my workplace, someone yelled at me, "You just need to fire him!" That was the participant's view, a loud one, and he was giving me advice.

As a leader, it is so easy to give advice as to what other people should do. In my line of work, I can see actions others could take pretty clearly, and I can even yell at them to take those actions. But until you, from your own view, see that the action will lead to the result you want, you probably won't do it. And even if you did, it likely won't yield the result if you aren't confident about it. If you are leading others through the exercise, your goal is 100 percent about the person you are coaching. All that matters is that *they* see it.

For many leaders, it matters that the next generation of leaders—the people who are going to replace us— are empowered and stand on the shoulders of what we have created. I work with many people who aren't measuring their success by their salaries; they're measuring it based on the legacy they're leaving behind.

Remember, though, others' idea of a legacy isn't necessarily the same as yours. If you tell your team you want them to be empowered, but then all bets are off the moment their idea of empowerment looks different from yours, you can have a disaster on your hands.

Sometimes we are conscious about our views, but sometimes we are not, because those views seem like facts to us. The truth is, as soon as you start thinking this person doesn't get it, they start believing they aren't the right person for the job. So, don't give advice. Instead, consider what would lead your colleagues or your employees to be successful? That's what you check in on—not your view of them. Don't make your leadership about your view, and don't make your view the truth or the only way to achieve results.

Check in Regularly

It's true—the Votta Exercise is about creating actions and structures that work for you or the person you are coaching—and I just told you not to give advice. However, there are times when one-on-one clients have asked to have coaching calls only when they need me, instead of holding weekly calls. It's not up to me to judge if the structures and actions put into place work best for the person I'm coaching. However, through experience, I know my coaching clients get a lot more traction when we talk on a regular basis, usually weekly, no matter how things are going.

Using the Votta Exercise regularly to intentionally move things along no matter where they're at leads to amazing results—ones I feel are more exponential because the client is continually looking for that next step toward achieving new results.

I recommend checking in with the person you are coaching at least once a quarter. Whether they are an entrepreneur or happily employed in a corporate job, part of the structure you establish as their coach could be seeing what jobs are open once a quarter. When working with me, my clients don't have to tell anyone else in the world they are looking at available job openings. I am a vault. Not only do I promise confidentiality,

I also promise anonymity. When they make a decision to look at what is available and choose not to leave that quarter, they are free to feel invested in their current situation and be more intentional about their actions during that quarter.

Handling Perfectionism

For people who are always looking for the perfect or "right" way to do things, it can feel debilitating when they don't have a clear path to that perfect result. Perfectionism could be impacting you in the workplace, either because you are a perfectionist, or you lead one. Perfectionists may take longer than others to complete a task. They may also avoid starting a task they do not feel confident in. They may feel the need to constantly achieve perfection, or view the end product as the most important part of any undertaking.

May Busch, author of *Accelerate: 9 Capabilities to Achieve Success at Any Career Stage* writes that perfectionism becomes a career-limiting behavior as you move up through the ranks. Her experience was that being a perfectionist manager was holding her back because she held everyone on her team up to her impossible standards. As a leader, you don't want perfectionism to get in the way of your progress, or the progress of the person you are coaching.

The Votta Exercise has made a huge difference for me as a self-proclaimed perfectionist. If you are a perfectionist, one of the most powerful obstacles standing in your way will be your view. Spend some time in step 2 and start noticing your view. When the voice in your head says things like, "If it's worth doing, it's worth doing right" or "This isn't good enough" or "Everything is riding on this", start separating these thoughts from the facts.

Taking a moment to look at all of the possible views to reach a goal not only helps to break up the sense that there is only one right way to view the goal, but it also ensures you are accepting input from others. Everyone loves this part the most in our public workshops, because they get ideas about actions and structures they don't already have in their head. By gathering input from others, you are able to produce better results in less time. Maybe the method or the actions are completely different from what you would have done with your own view, but ultimately, if you make the exercise about the result, then *how* the goal is achieved isn't as important. Given the kind of leader you want to be and the view you have created for yourself, it doesn't always matter how you get there. It only matters that you get there.

When you get to Step 5, Creating a Plan for Moving Forward, there are a number of actions you can implement or create to give yourself an 'out', so you don't get stuck in the perfectionism trap. For instance, you could give yourself a time limit on a task for yourself or a team member. Deadlines are great for this. You will complete the task whether or not you feel it is finished. If you have a tendency to strive for perfection in a task, then decide you will only spend 30 minutes (or a certain timeframe) on it. Set a timer and make it press "send" when time is up. Or, plan something really fun or something you *have* to go to when the time is up.

For example, one of my clients had to deliver an onboarding exercise to her direct supervisor and she was told that the exercise should take her two hours to complete. When she found herself at more than five hours and was nowhere near ready to submit, she reached out to me for coaching. She created a plan to give herself an additional hour on the task and submit it at the end of that hour, no matter what. When time was up, she wanted to keep working on it, but she wasn't getting paid for that additional time and had other urgent tasks to complete. In this case, I got on the phone with her as she submitted the exercise. She had fulfilled the intention of the task and got it off her plate.

As a perfectionist, I sometimes have the view that if people would just listen to me, everything would work out. Given that view, I take certain actions and I get certain results, but usually not the ones I want. The exercise is a great reminder for me when I have the view that *there is a right way to do it and my way is the right and only way, just in case we weren't sure*. When other people are allowed to have their views heard, people have more fun. When I approached issues with the angle of perfectionism and believed things had to be done in a certain way to have fun, usually no one had fun except for me. And sometimes, not even me.

Working collaboratively to make decisions or to have other people get on board with a certain result increases the effectiveness of the exercise. You want to invite as many views as possible. When many minds are focusing on the result and their chosen view, it makes it easier to achieve the goal. I gain more and more evidence for this claim as time passes.

The Votta Exercise can create freedom for the perfectionist. You don't necessarily have to lower your standards or values. Ask yourself what could be possible if you are willing to look from a different view.

Working with Family

If you want stuff to deal with all the time, then work with family. As I mentioned earlier, I work with my husband. Whether you work with actual family members or you have a created sense of family at your workplace, there is no shortage of opportunities to adjust your view.

Even in larger corporations when the next generation of leaders is being mentored to replace outgoing leadership, I often hear (confidentially), "I would never tell her this, but I see her as a daughter," or "I see him like a son." And we have all heard of the *work spouse*, a phrase referring to a coworker with whom one shares a special bond, similar to that of a marriage.

When you work with family—a spouse, a parent, adult children, a sibling—and you look back, sometimes there can be a lot there. Doing the Votta Exercise can be incredibly valuable, because sometimes it feels like you've got a short fuse, for lack of a better term. Something can happen that would be seemingly small with anyone else, but because your *sister* did it, your reaction is much bigger than it would have been otherwise.

I have been working with my husband off and on for as long as I've known him, which is over ten years. I love working with him. That said, we are most challenged when our views differ. My husband has a view that no one else works as hard as he does, and I happen to be "no one else". And I have a view that if something goes wrong, it's probably my fault. It really made a difference for us to do the exercise and recognize these opposing views and how they play out in our marriage. Each time we did the exercise, there was a different circumstance.

Creating goals was easy for us, as it was usually tied to our revenue. We lived together, and no one else was going to make money if we didn't. That was clear. Setting up initial structures was easy for us, too. We met weekly to define our actions going forward— one of which was to repeat step 4, look back, during each meeting.

It mattered to me that he viewed me as trustworthy; that if I promised an action or a result, I would follow through on that promise. When we first started working together, Kevin would get frustrated with me and say something like, "Kristin, you promised this and didn't do it." My response wasn't ever anything like, "Thank you for telling me." I wasn't nice, but I wasn't brutal. He is my husband, after all; I couldn't unleash on him and then go home because he was there at home, too.

Another part of our structure is to always have our coach support us. Our coach works with us both as a couple and as individuals to continue our personal growth and give us that outlet. It is really important, and it works for us. The structure we set up includes the freedom to choose how often we talk to our coach. Currently, Kevin talks to him once a month, and I talk to him once or twice a week. That's what works for us right now, but the structure has changed multiple times over the last decade.

Using a coach in this way is just an example of something that works for us. Please know that when I talk about working with family, I'm not telling you what we do so you can copy us. We definitely don't have all the answers; we want you to discover what works for you. The Votta Exercise is a tool to help you not only get clarity about how you want things to look, but also how to make them happen. Maybe you are delightful with your husband when he asks you why you didn't finish that thing you said you were going to do. I, on the other hand, am not.

Tying this all together, if you want a culture to work like it's a family, every single step of the Votta Exercise is helpful. You can't skip over any steps; with each step, you are consistently able to see things from different points of view.

As soon as you think you have somebody figured out, they might change. Remember, they could be growing, just like you are. Getting to know people is wonderful, and it is very helpful to remind yourself that if they are doing this work, change is still a constant.

People are always evolving. Are you still interacting with someone you hired five years ago the same way you did on day one? Also, if you work with family, it's good to remember your sister might not be the same person she was when she was six.

Don't Make Assumptions

Whether you've recently left corporate America to start your own business, or you have always worked as an entrepreneur, it's easy to assume other people see things the same way you see them. I do that all the time.

Of course, integrity matters. Of course, empowering people matters. Of course, being punctual matters. Most people would agree on those points. But if you were to ask every one of my family members, every one of my friends, and every one of my clients what it means to be punctual, you'd probably get a different answer from each and every one of them, because they all have their own view of what *punctual* means to them.

As a leader, you must do the work to create a specific agreement about what something means to you and the person you are working with—whether it's an employee, a colleague, or a client—which means putting it in writing and gathering signatures. Do everything it takes to avoid potential hassles and frustration down the road. If you happen to be doing business with family, you might think this isn't necessary. Do it anyway.

If you don't work to create a plan with specific actions and structures, put it in writing, and agree to the terms, you will regret it. The integrity of your business depends on it. As a coach, I don't often say people *have* to do something—I let them come to realizations on their own. But when working with a family member, you *have* to create a written agreement. In my book, it's not optional.

Setting Boundaries

Another issue that often comes up is the issue of boundaries and limits. The way I recommend establishing boundaries is that you don't find your limits, you create them. I've had clients in the past who have been hospitalized due to overworking themselves. That limit was created *for* them. We want you to create a boundary before it is made for you, and based on what is important to you.

For instance, I have a goal of making sure my family feels loved and needed. Setting boundaries for me looks something like this: *I just coached seven people on Tuesday. I know I can't do that again. I wasn't able to sleep. I had too much to do. I didn't spend any time with my family. I just can't do that.* That's different from thinking, *I'm choosing not to do that again, because though I can do it, it's not what works right now.* Again, I used my goals and views as a check and balance to see if my life is aligned with what really matters.

I choose to spend quality time with my family, and coaching seven clients in one day prevents me from meeting that goal. When I think of it this way, it allows me to be proud of the result. Having seven clients in one day is something to be proud of, too, but the two can't occur at the same time. Sure, I could choose to stay up late at night. But if wellbeing matters to you, it's not effective to stay up late. We choose our goals, prioritize them, and then set limitations based on what is most important to us. There are times when we have to get out of our own heads and have someone from the outside offer their perspective. This is where coaching can make a huge difference.

I'm a coach, and I also have a coach. I've had the same coach for eleven years, and he's helped me in various ways. Right now, I talk to him six times each month. There was a time when I talked to him only once a month. Whatever structure you start with can change when you need it to; it's worth checking in with yourself to figure your current needs and boundaries, especially when you're actively going through a transition.

I know some coaches and consultants say there is no such thing as work-life balance. I think your own version of work-life balance is all that matters. As with anything else, there are certain things that work for other people that can also work for you. It's worth investing the time and energy to do the exercise and figure out what those things are, and what they mean for you.

When you're working with family, it's too easy to blur the lines between your work and home life, especially if you have young children. I have many successful clients who don't need to use the exercise to make more money. They 100 percent use the exercise to create boundaries around their work and family life. They want to be able to close their computer at a certain time of day and focus on their kids. They use the exercise because they aren't able to figure it on their own. Since this balance is a priority for them, they use the exercise to put structures in place to make it happen. These folks are incredibly inspiring to me. My husband and I never had an issue with turning work off and turning our attention to the kids. I love talking about work, and so does my husband, so that was never part of the structure for us. But this is why structures are individual and beneficial. Everybody is different. What I thought was work-life balance a month ago, or maybe even a week ago, no longer pertains to my current situation. At the time of this writing, I have a six-year-old and a three-and-a-half year-old, and I'm sure it's no surprise our definition of balance changes by the day, if not by the hour.

Let's say you have a new goal of working forty hours a week and to avoid being on a screen outside office hours. That in and of itself can be a gigantic transition. What could a view of that be? It could be *It's not possible. There's no way. If I unplug from work, I'm going to lose my job.* There are plenty of possible views.

If we were to create any view for this, it could also be *It really is that easy. I shut my computer down, and I plug my phone into an outlet in the other room.* You pick whatever view you want of that goal. (And by the way, you also picked your goal. Remember why you picked that goal as you choose your view.) There is nobody dictating to you what the goal is when it comes to work-life balance. It is 100 percent whatever you create, and whatever you and your family create. Your view is just as unique as the goal. And remember, you couple the goal with the view you have chosen.

When work-life balance is your goal, it's common to be faced with a bunch of reasons why it might be difficult. This means there may be some things to clean up in the past. If you get frustrated, there *might* be some looking back to do around work-life balance. And that's okay. Going forward, there's a lot more flexibility available today than ever before. Many people are currently taking advantage of this, especially with the global shift to working from home brought on by the global pandemic. All you have to do is Google work-life balance, and you can find a lot of tips, tricks, and techniques on how this can work for you. I wouldn't do that, however, without first figuring out your view and your specific goal.

Work-life balance is attainable, especially during a big transition. You may be spending a lot of time at home right now. Maybe you are figuring out how to look for the job you want without settling for less. Or maybe you're wondering how to balance social time with friends and grandkids while also looking for another job, because you're not ready to retire yet. Or maybe you have retired from corporate America. Now what? It's worth figuring out what you want your transition to look like.

I'd like to add a note on productivity here. Remember all the different views of what *good* means? There are just as many interpretations for *productivity*, too. It is possible to rest. Taking time off in some cases can make you even more productive. But it depends on your view, and that can change over time. My husband, for example, finds no pleasure whatsoever in resting or recharging. He says that if he is not doing anything at home, he dwells on stuff that doesn't matter to him. He's not happy unless he's redesigning a room or planning our next vacation. A relax and recharge for him might look like "being busy" to other people.

His idea of a vacation is to be active, go on excursions, and fill every spare minute with activities. I'm like, "Can't I just sleep in?" We're very different. Knowing ourselves and those we care about will make times of big transition more manageable. But do the work on yourself, first.

It matters to me that my husband is happy and our relationship is happy, so we find value in doing this work with our coach. On a recent call with him, we realized we hadn't had any conversations lately about our 5-year plan. I was surprised. I help people figure out their next step, what makes them happy, fulfilled, and proud of themselves all the time. I help them set up structures so they can experience that joy. I do this for a living, but I still forget to check in with the people I love the most. That's why we have a coach. Left to my own devices, it could be a whole year before I have a conversation with my husband about what he wants life to look like. I thought, *You're the person I love the most in this world, and I haven't asked you.*

When it comes to work-life balance, I have more moments when I'm aware of what's going on in my life, and aware of what I am most proud of when I practice the Votta Exercise. That's a bonus my clients get, too, which isn't necessarily what they come to me for.

Intentionally Look for Things to Appreciate

I have a beautiful home office my husband built for me with his own two hands. I love it so much. He seemed to enjoy building it, and even got the kids involved to help. I see it as a very supportive, loving, and generous gesture.

The walls intentionally don't go to the ceiling. I have three beautiful windows in the office, and he didn't want it to be an oven in the summer. Makes sense, right? But it's almost useless for client calls, recording, and webinars right now. With the whole family home, including a new dog, I can hear every single sound.

However, I look into my new office and I am reminded of how much time and effort my husband put into the project. I'm looking for, and finding new ways to appreciate my life right now. For me, that means not ignoring the times I don't feel so appreciative, and setting up structures around the things that do matter to me.

I don't always feel that being appreciative comes naturally to me, no matter how much it *means* to me. And maybe more importantly, I don't innately know how others want to be appreciated. This is one of those areas I consider worth the effort, especially now.

It's worth it to do some planning and use my coach when needed.

When COVID hit in 2020, I took my half-day and full-day leadership workshops online. Since I could no longer use my office, I had to find a solution. I found that if I locked myself in the master bedroom and set my computer on a diaper box, it was the correct height for me to sit on the floor. And it had great lighting from the window, so I could host a virtual meeting or do virtual consulting.

One time, I was leading a webinar to teach the Votta Exercise during a leadership workshop, and I looked up to see my two children naked and banging on the window. It wasn't loud enough for the attendees to hear it, but I saw them giggling as they stood there, completely naked. There was no diaper or swimsuit to be found, and they were watching Mommy work. I love video conferencing because I can see everyone's faces, but at that moment I didn't love it, as the participants could see mine at that time. They couldn't see my kids, but they could see my facial expression, which said it all!

I had to pause the webinar quickly. I muted myself, paused, and yelled, "Where's Daddy?" And yes, their dad was on duty and nearby. He came right up and whisked them away. I am so thankful for the new fence (quarantine project #892), so my neighbors couldn't see my naked kids running around. And I had to continue the webinar as if nothing had happened. I was able to tell the participants one of my views was that I was horrified this was happening.

During the workshop, someone found a typo in a workbook, and I wanted to die. That was the worst thing ever. One of the views I had was *I'm faking it*. So, you can understand why sitting on the floor with my computer on a diaper box and my naked kids looking through the window was pretty much my worst nightmare. Luckily, I have structures around showing my vulnerability.

Thankfully, the participants on the webinar were very understanding, and I was able to quickly shift my view to *This is life now*, and that made a difference to me. I want to be the kind of leader who is transparent about what is going on in my life, so other people feel safe being transparent, too. There is no reason to pretend we aren't dealing with what is going on right now. Given the view *This is life now*, this experience became a cute and funny family anecdote. It was worth sharing with more people than just those on the webinar, because it matters to me that people are okay with the humanness of life exactly the way it is, and they are able to shift their view of it.

Two of the new views I have created are *people are able to be themselves around me*, and *they are accepted*. By sharing those moments, when a part of me could view it as a complete mistake or failure, I give other people the ability to be themselves around me. When people tell me I seem like I have my life together, it's a reminder to me that it's not real. I need to be vulnerable and share more about what my life is really like. By shifting that view, the actions are different.

I would not have shared if I was worried about being a failure. And by sharing, other people are able to exhale, share, and focus on what matters to them. One of my clients, a VP from a Fortune 50 company, hired me because I was so straightforward and forthright about my personal example. Sharing about how I used to drink allowed her to be comfortable sharing the things she is most vulnerable about. People hire me because they get to be themselves. Maybe they want something different from what they have right now, and that's okay. My naked children knocking on my window was an opportunity to share, and I want to be known for being real.

We are all dealing with unique circumstances. Pandemic or not, this is always the case. You may or may not be focusing on your growth as a leader, strategic partner, or tactical planner for your organization. The Votta Exercise, however, is useful for whatever situation you are in.

Creating the Life You Want

I hear more results from my clients every day. They are producing *facts* through using the Votta Exercise that inspire me every single day. Who these leaders are, and how they take on their own leadership to impact their lives, the lives of their families, their communities, and their organizations is what gets me out of bed in the morning.

Again, the Votta Exercise is reusable, reliable, and scalable. It is scalable because you can use it to impact large groups; but if there's a change that's going to happen, trust me, it starts with ourselves first. For example, let's say your leader just informed you the company is going to consolidate your department with another one. Yes, that will have a huge impact on lots of people, however, you'll have to work through the change yourself, first. How will the change affect you? How do you feel about it? What is your view? And what kind of person do you want to be over the course of the change? Only when you have resolved your own resistance to a change can you begin to effectively "control the pause" and plan the change management strategy for your department.

As you start experimenting with using the Votta Exercise tool, you may find you could benefit from additional guidance and support, and possibly hire a coach. If you are ready to learn new ways to implement and practice the Votta Exercise in your own life, visit AdjustYourView.com and check out my current coaching options. I would love to work with you.

Let's create the results you want in your life, in the ways you want, while being the leader you want to be.

Acknowledgements

Thank you to my husband, Kevin, for never doubting me about the things that really matter. You are a supportive partner and an extraordinary father. People don't always realize what a brilliant mind you have because you never flaunt it. It could be crushing for other people to learn that a man so good-looking is also self-aware, smart, and puts family first. And you can make me laugh—my honking laugh—no matter the situation. Thanks for pushing me forward to write this book. I needed those laughs many, many times.

To my crazy, sweet, smart kiddos, thank you for forcing me to reevaluate what's important over and over again. I love you so much. I look forward to learning more from you as you grow.

Thank you to my sister, my best friend, for talking me off a ledge when needed (many times throughout the process of writing this book), and loving me completely. I love you and your family so much.

My kids are fortunate enough to have nine grandparents. Some of them raised me, some of them raised my husband, and some of them joined the party a little later. To the ones that poured themselves into parenting me, I didn't exactly make it easy. I appreciate you all that much more now that I'm a parent. Thanks for teaching me that anything is possible, and that there's no one right way to accomplish things.

Thank you to the parental figures and mentors that adopted my family and me as your own. If you think I'm referring to you, I am. Your impact on me and my family has made a lasting, positive difference. You are family to us, too.

My early adopters—those of you who did my inaugural leadership programs and hired me to coach you or consult at your company—thank you. And to the more recent adopters, thank you for letting me partner with you to get the results you want, too. Without you, I would not be where I am today in my career, and definitely (obviously) would not have as many examples for this book. Don't worry, your names have been changed. Your trust means everything to me. You inspire me daily.

To my very first paying executive coaching client so long ago, thank you for asking me to coach you. You named your price (which was three times higher than what I would have asked for) and requested the highest level of confidentiality given your public role. It was an honor.

Thank you to my business networking friends. You make me feel much more popular than I may actually be. Yes, you've helped me grow my business, and I am so thankful. More than that, I appreciate your friendship. I've met some of the best people over the last decade.

I appreciate my friend and editor, Karen Rowe, for her expertise and energy! This book would not have been written any time this decade without her support, knowledge, and convenient humor throughout. Thank you to her whole team at Front Rowe Seat for making this a reality.

Thank you to my coach, EA Cross, for working with me for over a decade. You supported me as I navigated through much of my past I wasn't proud of, and you continue to work with me to grow my career and relationships. I am forever grateful to have you in my life.

About the Author

Kristin Votta is founder and executive coach of The Votta Group, a management consulting and leadership development firm headquartered in Tampa, Florida, with an international reach.

The Votta Group combines unique skills and experiences to deliver personal and professional value to individuals and complex business organizations that want value-driven results.

Kristin has been coaching leadership programs and facilitating seminars for over fifteen years. Kristin's training, experience, and sense of humor translate to a powerful experience, helping companies and leaders reach their goals quickly and effectively.

When you meet her, you'll quickly learn she is the first to laugh at her own jokes and share vulnerable stories with the hope of making even strangers feel comfortable around her.

Active in her community, Kristin is thankful to serve on non-profit boards and fundraise for various local charities. She is happily married with two young children, two cats, and a rescued English Pointer who is scared of the cats.

Notes

[1] https://medium.com/the-philosophers-stone/why-existentialism-is-the-only-philosophy-that-makes-any-sense-86beca9e8c48

[2] https://blog.oup.com/2013/11/correlation-is-not-causation/

[3] https://towardsdatascience.com/why-correlation-does-not-imply-causation-5b99790df07e

[4] https://thriveglobal.com/stories/do-you-view-the-reality-of-your-world-through-a-lens/

[5] https://www.smithsonianmag.com/science-nature/how-our-brains-make-memories-14466850/

[6] https://www.techexplorist.com/human-brain-works-reverse-order-retrieve-memories/20134/

[7] https://www.newstatesman.com/politics/education/2016/02/head-cloud

[8] https://www.newstatesman.com/politics/education/2016/02/head-cloud

[9] Hunt, Vivian; Prince, Sara; Dixon-Fyle, Sundiatu; Yee, Lareina. "Delivering through Diversity." McKinsey & Company, January 2018, 14. https://www. mckinsey.com/~/media/McKinsey/Business percent20Functions/Organization/Our percent20Insights/Delivering percent20through percent20diversity/ Delivering-through-diversity_full-report.ashx

[10] https://maybusch.com/8-ways-stop-being-perfectionist/

CPSIA information can be obtained
at www.ICGtesting.com
Printed in the USA
BVHW041146010421
603931BV00010B/849